www.wadsworth.com

wadsworth.com is the World Wide Web site for Wadsworth Publishing Company and is your direct source to dozens of online resources.

At *wadsworth.com* you can find out about supplements, demonstration software, and student resources. You can also send e-mail to many of our authors and preview new publications and exciting new technologies.

wadsworth.com
Changing the way the world learns®

ETHICS ON THE JOB
CASES AND STRATEGIES

Second Edition

Raymond S. Pfeiffer
Delta College

Ralph P. Forsberg
Delta College

Wadsworth Publishing Company
I⟨T⟩P® An International Thomson Publishing Company

*Belmont, CA • Albany, NY • Boston • Cincinnati • Johannesburg
London • Madrid • Melbourne • Mexico City • New York
Pacific Grove, CA • Scottsdale, AZ • Singapore • Tokyo • Toronto*

Philosophy Editor: Peter Adams
Assistant Editor: Kerri Abdinoor
Editorial Assistant: Mindy Newfarmer
Marketing Manager: Dave Garrison
Project Editors: Michelle Provorny,
     Rita Jaramillo
Print Buyer: Stacey Weinberger

Permissions Editor: Bob Kauser
Creative Director: Stephen Rapley
Copyeditor: Laura Larson
Cover Design: Stanton Design
Compositor: R & S Book Composition
Printer: Webcom

For permission to use material from this text, contact us:
      web   www.thomsonrights.com
      fax   1-800-730-2215
      phone   1-800-730-2214

Printed in Canada
     4 5 6 7 8 9 10

Wadsworth Publishing Company
10 Davis Drive
Belmont, CA 94002

International Thomson Editores
Seneca, 53
Colonia Polanco
11560 México D.F. México

International Thomson Publishing Europe
Berkshire House
168-173 High Holborn
London, WC1V 7AA, United Kingdom

International Thomson Publishing Asia
60 Albert Street #15-01
Albert Complex
Singapore 189969

Nelson ITP, Australia
102 Dodds Street
South Melbourne
Victoria 3205 Australia

International Thomson Publishing Japan
Hirakawa-cho Kyowa Building, 3F
2-2-1 Hirakawa-cho, Chiyoda-ku
Tokyo 102, Japan

Nelson Canada
1120 Birchmount Road
Scarborough, Ontario
Canada M1K 5G4

International Thomson Publishing Southern Africa
Building 18, Constantia Square
138 Sixteenth Road, P.O. Box 2459
Halfway House, 1685 South Africa

Library of Congress Cataloging-in-Publication Data
Pfeiffer, Raymond S.
    Ethics on the job: cases and strategies/Raymond S. Pfeiffer, Ralph P. Forsberg.—2nd ed.
        p.   cm.
      ISBN 0-534-57300-2 (pbk.)
      1. Business ethics.   I. Forsberg, Ralph P.   II. Title.
    HF5387.P45   1999
    174'.4—dc21

We dedicate this text to our mothers and fathers, who taught us that doing right is its own reward.

CONTENTS

GUIDE TO TOPICS IN CASES

Advertising/marketing: 18, 21, 32

Affirmative action: 17

Competition: 9, 41, 42, 44

Computer use: 9, 10, 21, 42

Corporate responsibility: 8, 13, 17, 18, 19, 21, 24, 27, 32, 35, 36, 41, 45

Discrimination: 12, 13, 14, 15, 16, 17, 18, 19, 20, 26, 33, 45

Diversity/relations with other cultures: 17, 18, 19, 26, 33, 43

Employer-employee relations: 1, 4, 5, 6, 7, 8, 12, 13, 14, 15, 16, 20, 22, 23, 24, 26, 28, 29, 30, 31, 34, 40, 43, 45

Employee rights: 1, 4, 5, 6, 7, 11, 12, 13, 15, 16, 17, 19, 20, 22, 23, 24, 26, 30, 31, 34, 37, 38, 43, 45

Environment and pollution: 35, 41

Finance: 25, 38

Firing/termination/downsizing: 4, 7, 11, 12, 15, 16, 24, 30, 45

Government regulation: 17, 19, 28, 29, 32, 36, 37, 38, 41

Hiring: 1, 2, 3, 13, 35, 43

Information access: 1, 4, 9, 10, 21, 34, 37, 38, 40, 42 Insider information: 5, 9, 10, 38, 42

Insider trading: 38

The law: 6, 13, 14, 15, 17, 19, 20, 21, 22, 25, 28, 31, 32, 36, 37, 38, 40, 41, 44, 45

Obligations to employees 3, 4, 5, 6, 7, 8, 12, 13, 14, 23, 24, 26, 28, 30, 31, 34, 45

Obligations to one's employer: 2, 6, 7, 9, 10, 22, 27, 28, 29, 31, 32, 37, 40, 42

PREFACE TO SECOND EDITION

The conviction that led us to write the first edition of this book has neither weakened nor altered significantly in the ensuing years. It is above all the belief that much can be gained from the study of practical, applied ethical decision making. Indeed, such study has benefits for the student that differ from those of a more philosophical approach to the subject. Chief among them are a working grasp of ethical principles and reasoning in day-to-day decision making. Our students have commented to us time and again that study of the RESOLVEDD strategy through practice in applying its main components to personal ethical problems is the most useful and rewarding part of their study of ethics.

This book has, somewhat unexpectedly, brought to the market no rival to the RESOLVEDD strategy, no new decision-making strategy designed to guide students through the basic and most important parts of an analysis leading directly to a decision in the face of ethical conflict. The book continues to be the only supplementary ethics text devoted completely to teaching people a strategy for ethical decision making.

The years of use since writing the book have brought to our attention the need for improvement in a number of areas. Some cases in the first edition seemed to grow tired with time, and some became irrelevant in our students' eyes. New ethical problems involving, for example, such omnipresent topics as office gossip, nepotism, union negotiations, sexual harassment and abuse, price gouging, environmental conflicts and international business have arisen in interest both in the popular press and among the general population. We have developed new cases to address these issues in ways designed to help sensitize students to their presence and relevance in their daily lives.

In addition, we have sharpened many of our older cases that had fundamentally sound approaches. In the main, we have tried to revise them in a way which clarifies the value choices they bring forth. We have tried to retain the names and numbers of cases that are either the same as those contained in the first edition or revisions of cases contained in the first edition. Some of the revised cases have been changed extensively. We have added twelve new cases that did not appear in the first edition. Together, the extensively revised and new cases comprise twenty-seven of the forty-five cases in the second edition.

The following list identifies unchanged, revised, and new cases:

Unchanged: 1, 2, 3, 5, 6, 7, 8, 9, 10, 11, 13, 15, 16, 17, 32, 36, 41, 42

Revised: 12, 14, 19, 20, 23, 25, 27, 28, 29, 30, 31, 33, 37, 38, 40

New: 4, 18, 21, 22, 24, 26, 34, 35, 39, 43, 44, 45

For users of our first edition who do not see their favorite cases in the second edition, we hope to have them available soon over the Internet or on CD-ROM.

We have reformulated the leading case in the book to make it a more typical kind of ethical problem for a lower-level manager. The new case of "Your Subordinate" illustrates how ethical values and principles can play a role in the most common and prosaic of business decisions. The analysis of it, which is fully drawn out in Chapter 3, is designed to help students understand more clearly the distinction between the evaluation and the values stages of the analysis. It has been this distinction more than any other in the strategy that has given our students difficulty.

Our lack in the first edition of any clear section on the ethics of capitalism often caused our students to go elsewhere for an understanding of this topic. We gradually came to see that ethical decision making in the workplace requires an understanding of the market; its reliance on trust, truth, and competition; and its dependence on society's approval to recognize a limited right to own personal property. We have included a new section in the present edition to provide a working perspective for ethical decision makers applying the RESOLVEDD strategy in earnest.

The sections in the first edition on the rights to make a profit and own property and the rights of future generations were misleading for many students, so they have been deleted. The important points of those sections have been included in the new section on the ethics of capitalism. A number of other sections in the first five chapters have been extensively revised, but the book remains largely unchanged in its basic format.

ACKNOWLEDGMENTS

The first edition of this book was born of the growing awareness among teachers of applied ethics that ethical decision making involves ways of thinking that differ in significant respects from those appropriate to the philosophical study of ethics. The first edition brought to fruition many ideas and lessons growing out of a long process of reflection, dialogue, and experimentation spurred on by the commitment to improve the value of our teaching for our students. The second edition continues to respond to the same concerns, as well as to incorporate new issues and respond to comments from students about weaknesses in the first edition.

Raymond Pfeiffer first became aware of the need for a decision-making strategy when teaching bioethics to Delta College nursing students in 1979. He found that ethical theories traditionally studied in courses in philosophical ethics have limited value for making decisions in everyday contexts. Professor Richard A. Wright, a consultant sponsored by the National Endowment for the Humanities, suggested the importance of offering a practical strategy for students to apply when confronting ethical issues on the job. Pfeiffer's attempts to use Wright's own Situation Assessment Procedure led him to develop an early version of the decision-making strategy presented here. He initially used *DIAGNOSE* as an acronym to help students master the steps of the strategy. Although the strategy worked well, Pfeiffer was not fully satisfied with the acronym. A colleague, Max Thomas, suggested, in 1987, that *SOLVE* might be adapted as a better acronym. This word had other shortcomings, which were later addressed in developing the acronym *RESOLVEDD* as it is presented here.

Ralph Forsberg's teaching of applied ethics at Harper College, Ripon College, and Loyola University of Chicago had led him to become aware of the limitations of many of the cases presented by texts in business ethics. Typically, they required the student to assume the role of a top executive or owner of a company. He undertook, beginning in the early 1980s, to develop cases that would be more typical of the kinds of employment his students would have during college and in the first few years beyond. He found important encouragement in this endeavor from Professors Patricia A. Werhane and David T. Ozar at Loyola. He also acknowledges the valuable conversations about business and ethics he has had with his special friends, Frank Flasch and Kate Flasch, both accomplished businesspeople.

When the authors became colleagues at Delta College in 1989, they discovered the complementary nature of their interests, which continues to the present.

We owe a special debt to Bernard Gert's work. We have found a version of his notion of the moral rules to be helpful in applying the RESOLVEDD strategy. We have not, however, adopted all of his moral rules or the precise formulations of those rules that emerge from his careful and insightful analysis.

Our students in medical ethics and business ethics classes over the past decade have helped us sharpen and season our approach. Mary Sue Anderson, Michelle Cobb, Cassandra Collier, Steven W. May, Raquel L. Mondol, Cynthia L. Ott, and James A. Wood have graciously allowed us to adapt their ideas and writings for this work.

The free and open environment at Delta College has contributed immeasurably to the development of this book. Our colleague in philosophy, Professor Linda Plackowski, was of special help. Many of our colleagues in the divisions of nursing, business, social science, humanities, technology, and allied health have reviewed our ideas; some have encouraged us to try them out on their students. In particular, Professors Alan Hill, Sharon Lehrer, Paul Hill, Jessie Dolson, Louise Goodburne, Bruce Leppien, Ion Keefer, and John Flattery have provided time, energy, thoughts, and opportunities to work with their students, and they deserve our special gratitude.

The philosophy editor at Wadsworth at the time of our first edition, Ken King, was an important source of encouragement and guidance. The present philosophy editor, Peter Adams, has continued that tradition and has caused us to broaden our horizons. The professors who reviewed the manuscript for Wadsworth and ITP made many insightful suggestions that helped us improve the final product significantly. Our thanks to: Cyril Dwiggins, Dickinson College; Ida M. Jones, California State University—Fresno; John L. Longeway, University of Wisconsin—Parkside; Michael S. Pritchard, Western Michigan University; George L. Stengren, Central Michigan University; Art Wolfe, Michigan State University.

Like other textbook authors, we owe a debt to the many thinkers from whom we have shamelessly borrowed and adapted many ideas and approaches. Our work has grown from participation in an extended community of teachers, scholars, and philosophers whose integrity and wisdom have inspired and motivated us. It would be impossible to fully credit all of these people, for which we apologize.

CHAPTER 1

ETHICS AND ETHICAL DECISION MAKING

1.1 A PERSONAL ETHICAL PROBLEM: THE CASE OF YOUR SUBORDINATE

The hourly employees at Korry Manufacturing are protected by a union contract with an appeals process and a provision for binding arbitration. As a shift supervisor, you work hard to motivate your subordinates as best you can, although you have little success with Grindel, a senior worker who is minimally competent but is effective at standing up for his rights. Now in his mid-fifties, Grindel will not likely retire for another decade, protected as he is by the union. He operates a punch press and produces more than twice the average rate of defective parts. Your discussions and offers to provide him more training have brought forth nothing but refusal, obstinacy, and the insistence that his work is not below union standards.

Your supervisor knows and detests Grindel, and his coworkers seem to like him no better. He is often the butt of their jokes, but he has no real negative effect on them and has never been the object of their complaints. Although he is not a major problem for Korry, your boss has repeatedly viewed him as a problem you should address, recommending that you "shake off that dead wood."

Your boss has recently suggested that you take steps to motivate Grindel to seek employment elsewhere. He has encouraged you to move him around more often among the least desirable jobs and to assign him to an inconvenient swing shift for a couple of weeks. Such treatment is entirely legal and not forbidden by the union contract. However, if you do this, it will surely be noticed and easily documented. What should you do in response to your boss's demand?

Such a situation would present you with a personal ethical problem. Whatever you do, you must choose. Whether you recognize it or not, ethical values are at stake. If you do nothing, you have chosen a course of action with consequences. You have decided against taking steps likely to benefit your employer. Your refusal to act appears to indicate that your duty to your employer has less importance in your eyes than some other considerations.

If, on the other hand, you move to carry out your boss's suggestions, you are clearly causing harm to Grindel and treating him in an underhanded and less than fully honest way. You are sacrificing your commitment to fair treatment and perhaps your reputation. You are following what may be your duty to your employer at the expense of your own commitment to forthrightness or other values you personally hold to be important. Because of the complexities and values at stake, such a situation may present you with an agonizing choice.

This book offers a strategy that will help you respond to such personal ethical problems. A perfect solution to such a problem would be one in which you violate no ethical values and yet achieve your most important goals. However, when perfect solutions are unavailable, one must settle for the best of the alternatives. The decision-making strategy developed in this book will show you how to address a number of questions that can help you find the best solution.

To make a responsible decision, you should consider the choices available, the outcomes of each, and their likely impacts on people's lives. Just which ethical values are upheld and which are violated by the alternatives are essential factors. Which of these values are important for your decision and which are unimportant must be carefully weighed. How upholding or violating certain values affects your own sense of integrity and your character also have to be considered. Whether your ethical values are more important than some of your other personal goals may present a further challenge.

We assume that ethical values are important to each of us and that we want to make decisions that compromise these values as little as reasonably possible. The process of evaluating and choosing among our ethical values, our personal goals, and the likely consequences of our actions is far from simple. However, this process is clarified and facilitated by use of the RESOLVEDD strategy of decision making presented in Chapter 3.

The purpose of the RESOLVEDD strategy is to help you arrive at decisions that implement an ethical point of view. Consideration of certain basic aspects of such a viewpoint may help you understand the spirit of the strategy. The purpose of pursuing the RESOLVEDD strategy is, in short, to arrive at a decision by which you achieve your most important goals while compromising ethical values as little as reasonably and ethically justifiable. Everyone must weigh such decisions from their own personal point of view and against the background of their own ethical beliefs. From whatever set of personal values or beliefs we view ethical decisions, the RESOLVEDD strategy can clarify the *process* by which we apply our values. The strategy does not presuppose any particular ethical theory or perspective but is designed to be helpful procedurally, regardless of the theory or perspective we hold.

1.2 ETHICS, JUDGMENTS, PRINCIPLES AND VALUES

Ethics may be viewed as the study of the justification of ethical value judgments. An *ethical value judgment* is a judgment of right or wrong, good or bad, better or worse, virtue or vice, or what ought or ought not to be done. Justification involves giving reasons or evidence for the truth or falsehood of a given judgment.

Consider the following value judgment as it applies to the Case of Your Subordinate:

I have a duty to do what my superior tells me to do.

To determine the likely truth or falsehood of such a judgment, you would examine the evidence for and against it. To cite and evaluate such evidence would be to proceed within the discipline of ethics.

Ethical principles are commonly used to justify ethical judgments. In the effort to justify the previous value judgment, you might state:

Employees have a duty to follow the orders of their superiors.

This is an ethical principle. It makes an ethical value judgment about a range of cases, not simply one particular situation. Ethical principles are important because we use them as reasons to think that a given decision or more specific value judgment is a good one or not so good.

People often refer to their ethical principles as ethical values. "It is against my values to treat an employee in such a nasty, sneaky way" may mean simply that treating an employee that way violates some of the ethical principles you take seriously. The terms *ethical values* and *ethical principles* are used almost interchangeably throughout this text.

People at times disagree about ethical values. Such disagreement may come from a number of sources. There may, for example, be disagreement over the proper formulation of ethical principles. Thus, you might disagree with the prior principle on the grounds that employees do not have a duty to follow orders that are ethically objectionable. Next, people sometimes disagree over whether and how an ethical principle applies to a specific situation. You might argue that although that principle is true, it does not apply to the Case of Your Subordinate because your boss did not give you a direct order to do anything but merely suggested it to you. People also may disagree over the question of which ethical principles are most important in a given situation. You might argue that the principle stated earlier is not nearly as important as the principle that people have a duty not to violate the rights of a worker. This principle may well be argued to pertain directly to the case because moving Grindel around as suggested is a clear violation of his right to be treated fairly, openly, honestly and to be informed of management's opinion of him.

1.3 AN ETHICAL POINT OF VIEW: THE PRINCIPLE OF EQUAL CONSIDERATION OF INTERESTS

We assume that you want to improve your ability to make ethical value judgments. We assume, too, that you want to approach personal ethical problems from an ethical point of view. Such a point of view is expressed by the principle of equal consideration of interests (ECI), which may be summarized as follows:

> You should make judgments and decisions and act in ways that treat the interests and well-being of others as no less important than your own.[*]

ECI does not imply that ethical behavior means treating the interests and well-being of others as more important than your own or that you never take your own interests into account. Rather, it implies fairness and impartiality in your dealings with other people. It requires, for example, that you not move Grindel around as suggested largely because you dislike him. It requires that your own personal likes and dislikes not count as reasons to think something is right or wrong, or ought or ought not to be done. It also requires that you count your own interests as equal to the interests of others, neither more nor less important than theirs.

ECI requires that you use your ethical principles as reasons and that you apply these principles equally to yourself and to others. If you believe it would be wrong for a manager to move you around in the manner suggested for Grindel, then you should oppose moving Grindel and others around in that manner. Whether you are a manager or a worker like Grindel, and whether he is a worker or manager is irrelevant to the ethical reasons that treating him in such a manner may be wrong. The ethical person applies ethical principles impartially, recognizing the equal moral value of the lives and well-being of all persons.

An ethical decision, then, is a decision that (1) implements an ethical point of view, not violating ECI; (2) compromises ethical principles as little as reasonably and ethically justifiable; and (3) allows you to achieve your personal goals to as great an extent as consistent with 1 and 2.

1.4 CONFLICTING GOALS

Our personal goals sometimes conflict with our ethical value judgments. In deciding what to do about Grindel, you might think that on ethical grounds you should not move him around but that failing to do so might end up costing you your job. Furthermore, the job may in fact be important to you. This sort of personal conflict must be taken seriously and may be addressed by several strategies.

First, you should investigate the nature of the possible threat to your personal goals. How real is that threat? Are you protected by a union contract or by any regulations or management policies in Korry? Are there policies that provide you due process before being fired? Could you persuade your supervisor of other more preferable steps? Could some sort of compromise be reached? Could you obtain support from your supervisor or some other person in a position of authority? Further investigation might reveal that the risk to your job is minimal.

Second, you should investigate the weight and firmness of your ethical beliefs in the situation. Is the suggested treatment of Grindel clearly unethical? How seriously so?

---

[*]Peter Singer, *Practical Ethics* (Cambridge: Cambridge University Press, 1979), 19.

Third, you should consider the importance of your personal goals in the case. How much ambition do you have for your career at Korry? What is worth sacrificing to pursue that career? Is it more important than your conscience or your reputation?

Fourth, you should calculate the chances of success in proceeding to act on your ethical convictions. Can you formulate an alternate and clearly preferable solution to the one suggested? Are you likely to be successful in persuading your boss of your view of the subject? Who else might support you, why, and how might you obtain such support?

Fifth, you will likely benefit by discussing the issues with other people. Such discussions may reveal unnoticed options, new information, different perspectives, and alternate value judgments and may expand your understanding and grasp of the issues. As a result, you may be more likely to arrive at a decision in which you can have confidence.

A responsible decision should not ignore your own legitimate or ethically defensible personal goals. To the extent that our goals in life are legitimate, we owe it to ourselves to take them seriously. Ethics does not require us to ignore self-interest or make personal sacrifices for trivial or ill-considered reasons. Again, we must weigh our own interests as equal to those of others, neither ignoring ourselves nor giving extra weight to our own interests.

The goal of the RESOLVEDD strategy of ethical decision making, introduced in Chapter 3, is to help you arrive at decisions with which you can live—in the full sense. An ethical decision is one in which you can take pride and willingly explain to others. The study of ethical decision making can help you maintain your integrity and live with a clear conscience.

1.5 ETHICAL JUSTIFICATION

Decision making in a situation with a personal ethical problem should be based on assessment of the evidence for and against the various options. Study of this evidence reveals which option is most clearly justified. Justification thus refers to the evidence for and against a given judgment. Ethical decision making requires that you judge the significance of the evidence to arrive at the most clearly justified choice given the circumstances.

Two main kinds of reasons can be offered as evidence to justify an ethical decision. You can offer reasons based on the effects of the decision and reasons based on relevant ethical principles. A responsible decision regarding a personal ethical problem should emerge from careful evaluation of both kinds of reasons both for and against all the available options.

In the Case of Your Subordinate, you might argue that your duty to uphold the right to fair and open treatment of employees requires you to seek some other solution to your problem. If so, you are citing the right to fair and open treatment of employees as an important ethical principle that should be upheld. Because this principle is relevant to the case, it may be offered as a reason to think it is justifiable not to follow your supervisor's suggestion. Of course, you would need to state clearly just what that principle is, and you might need to check on the considerations supporting it.

Another reason not to move Grindel around as suggested might be that doing so may lead to certain important, undesirable consequences. Grindel might in time figure out that he is being treated this way by design and file a grievance with the union. As the word spreads among his coworkers, they might well resent the treatment he is receiving and come to resent you as well. This reaction might in turn lead to a loss of your effectiveness as a manager. Such a situation might be bad for Korry as well as for you.

In making any decision, it is important to identify and evaluate both the relevant ethical principles and consequences. In the RESOLVEDD strategy, the consequences are to be identified in steps 4 and 5 and the principles in step 6. There is no simple procedure for conducting an evaluation of the relevant reasons for and against a given option. However, some reasons are better than others, and this difference can be discerned by comparing and contrasting the options and the principles and consequences that support them. The task of doing this is the seventh step in the RESOLVEDD strategy, explained in Chapters 3 and 4 and illustrated in Chapter 5.

1.6 ETHICAL VALUES: JUSTIFIABLE EXCEPTIONS

Ethical values are principles that help us make decisions implementing the ethical point of view. Ethicists largely agree that any principle must have three characteristics for it to be an ethical principle for a given person: the principle must be important to the person, the person must believe that all people should treat it as important, and the person must believe that it should be applied in accordance with the principle of Equal Consideration of Interests.

First, for a given principle to be someone's ethical principle, it should be important to that person. That is, it should be important enough to override some of that person's personal preferences. If honesty is one of your ethical principles, then you are willing to avoid deceiving others even if it causes you personal inconvenience. A person who is willing to lie for a petty gain is one for whom honesty is probably not truly an ethical value.

Second, for a given principle to be someone's ethical principle, the person should believe that other people should also live in accordance with it. This requirement rules out many uniquely personal preferences. Thus, one person's preference for Blue Moon–flavored ice cream is probably not an ethical principle for that person. As much as one may prize that flavor of ice cream, one's preference is not one of one's ethical values or principles unless one believes earnestly that all people have an obligation to prefer it.

On the other hand, people ordinarily believe that their ethical principles are principles that others should follow. Those who prize honesty typically believe that other people should prize it, too. They act in accordance with their own ethical principles in the firm belief that the world would generally be a better place if all people acted in accordance with those principles.

Finally, for a principle to be an ethical principle for a given person, that person must believe that it should be followed by him- or herself (and others) in a way that implements the principle of ECI. If honesty is one of your ethical principles, then you will not be honest merely when convenient. Doing so would be to treat the interests of others as less important than your own.

These three requirements do not imply that an ethical principle should never be violated. Situations may arise in which it is impossible to act in ways that do not violate any ethical principles. You might find yourself in a situation in which every option violates either the principle of truth (that you should not deceive people) or the principle of harm (that you should not do things that harm people). If so, you must choose between the options and thus violate one of these principles. To act ethically, you will try to choose which option violates which principle more seriously, and which upholds which principle more seriously. Such a situation is sometimes called a *lose-lose situation.* Such choices are discussed more in Chapters 3 and 4 and are illustrated in Chapter 5.

Although ethical principles are important, one need not assume that they are universally inviolable or absolute. It is possible, although controversial, to recognize the importance of certain ethical principles and to implement an ethical point of view without maintaining that any principles make absolute, unexceptionable, or inviolable demands on your life. An ethical principle may be important even if you recognize certain ethically justifiable exceptions to it. To recognize the existence of such exceptions is not necessarily to reduce the importance of that ethical principle. If you recognize exceptions (such as capital punishment or euthanasia) to the principle that one should not kill people, you may still object just as strongly to the murder of an innocent, blameless individual. Whether you recognize capital punishment or euthanasia as ethically justifiable is irrelevant to the question of how wrong it is to murder an innocent person.

Whether ethical principles are absolute is in one sense irrelevant to ethical decision making. To act ethically, you must have ethical principles, recognize their importance, follow them unless there is clear and strong ethical justification not to do so in a specific case, and apply them consistently, equally, and fairly in all of your relations to others. Whether those principles are peculiar to yourself or widely held in society or the world, or whether you believe they make absolute, unexceptionable demands on you need not be answered to make responsible ethical decisions in specific cases.

1.7 WHY SHOULD I ACT ETHICALLY?

This is one of the great questions of philosophical ethics that has been addressed by many of the great philosophers, beginning with Socrates, Plato, and Aristotle. A full answer is outside the scope of this book. However, it is worth noting briefly one direction such an answer might take.

To act ethically is, at the very least, to strive to act in ways that do not hurt other people; that respect their dignity, individuality, and uniquely moral value; and that treat others as equally important to oneself. If you believe these are worthwhile goals, then you have reason to strive to act ethically. If you do not believe these are worthwhile goals for human beings to pursue, then you may believe that it is not important to act ethically.

Those who renounce the importance of ethics either renounce these goals completely or believe that such goals can just as well be pursued on occasion, when convenient, to maintain appearances, and can just as well be ignored when inconvenient. Probably very few people renounce such goals altogether. A lifestyle characterized by complete lack of ethical behavior would be so antisocial that it might well result in imprisonment or social ostracism.

Many people, however, seem to think that they can live their lives in ways that are ethical much of the time but unethical at other times. Such an intermittently unethical lifestyle has many pitfalls, some of which are worth listing briefly here:

1. Such a lifestyle, when discovered by others, usually leads them to lose trust in the person.

2. Those who discover such behavior sometimes seek to retaliate against the offenders.

3. Living in such ways sometimes leads people to act unethically at the wrong time. We all rely on our habits and inclinations when there is too little time to deliberate. Unethical behaviors weaken our inclinations to act ethically and may lead us, in times of stress, to act in ways we later regret.

4. Living in such ways may make us feel guilty if we have been brought up in families and societies that established in us a sense of conscience.

5. Acting ethically only at selected times leads us to lose trust in ourselves. As a result, we may become worried, unsure, and anxious about the possibility that we may make a mistake and act unethically at the wrong times.

6. Acting unethically, when we choose, leads us to occasional violations of many values that are important to us, such as those presented in the next chapter. It leads us to violate honesty, loyalty, consistency, fairness, and many other important ethical principles.

7. The intermittently unethical lifestyle may violate our religious beliefs.

In summary, the intermittently unethical lifestyle may lead to a life of more misery than the ethical lifestyle. Of course, this point does not prove conclusively that each of us will live better if we strive to act ethically all of the time. Whether that is true is a matter each person must judge as life progresses. However, in making such choices, we should not ignore the lessons provided from the cultural, religious, literary, and moral traditions in which we live. Our values have emerged from those traditions and are deeply enmeshed in them. They may shed important light on the hard decisions we face in life.

1.8 THE CONTEXT OF ETHICAL DECISION MAKING IN BUSINESS: ELEMENTS OF A CAPITALIST SYSTEM

In America today, capitalism is the economic system within which business operates. Throughout the world, more and more countries have abandoned other economic models to embrace the capitalist way of doing business. Although some countries still exist in which capitalism does not dominate (for example, Cuba), even those countries must work within the capitalist system when conducting international business. And even in organizations that are not businesses, many of the values and principles of capitalistic businesses play a guiding role. To address ethical issues in workplaces, it is essential to recognize the main principles and values of capitalism.[*] Those that are most relevant to ethical questions include profit, the institution of private property, competition, and the concept of fairness or justice.

Profit

Profit is simply the amount of money a company or individual earns in excess of the costs of doing business. That is, once the costs of raw materials, wages, production, and other elements necessary to produce a product or deliver a service are covered, profit is what remains of the income from sales over and beyond this amount. Within the capitalist framework there are many reasons and justifications for allowing people and corporations to acquire profit. Without the profit motive and the freedom to pursue profit, capitalism does not exist.

To recognize that in a capitalist system, businesses exist to make a profit is not to say that profit is the only reason they exist. Although profit is a major motivator for those owning and operating businesses, society permits businesses to exist because it wants the services and products the businesses provide. Society views the profit motive as an effective means to promote work and innovation.

The profit motive itself is the desire of the owners and operators of business for monetary gain over time. Generally, a company is economically successful only to the extent that its profit margin increases. Companies whose profit margins remain level or fall are headed for financial trouble. Investors want to see increases in profit margins, and they accept a degree of risk in exchange for potential of growth in profit. In the capitalist system, companies granted the right to exist are given the right to make a profit as long as they obey the actual laws in effect. An economic system that does not allow businesses to make and keep a significant proportion of their profits is not a capitalist system.

The justification for permitting the existence of profit making begins with the argument that those who put forth and thus risk their own resources deserve the benefits of the venture once they have fulfilled their contractual agreements and paid their employees. However, the funds that remain after payment of these contracts and other expenses are profits and belong properly to the owners and investors. If a business enterprise fails, it is the investors who suffer the burden of losing their resources. Employees lose their jobs but are free to find employment elsewhere. Because investors back business enterprises for the explicit purpose of making a profit and take considerable risks in doing so, they have a right to the profits that accrue.

Other considerations can be cited to justify the existence of profit. Corporate profits are measures of a company's success. Reports of profit are indicators of effectiveness and promote intelligent investments. In most cases, increases in profit

---

*The analysis here owes much to Marshall Missner's book *Ethics of the Business System* (Van Nuys, CA: Alfred, 1980).

require a combination of high-quality product and low production costs combined with increasingly satisfied customers. Individual workers must acquire the skills in demand and use those skills appropriately. The quest for profit also encourages creativity in the development of new products, marketing, and all aspects of sales and production. Finally, a profitable company is more likely to reinvest in the economy in ways that create jobs and other benefits for society.

It is important to understand the reasoning that justifies limitations on profit. Governments routinely tax business profits, for reasons widely thought to be justifiable. Businesses exist at the discretion of government and for the benefit of society. Tax revenues may be used to benefit society in ways that businesses otherwise would not. These revenues may be used to maintain a business environment that fosters competition and thus promotes socially beneficial business activities. Moreover, business practices that are judged not to benefit society may, as a result, be regulated, limited, or outlawed. Profit making is thus widely thought to be justifiably limited by the well-being of society. Within such legal and ethical limits, however, profit making is an accepted and necessary practice in capitalist economies.

In the capitalist marketplace every participant seeks some sort of financial gain. Consumers gain by shopping for bargains and comparing competitors' prices for equal quality and quantity of products. The workers gain from higher wages, greater benefits, or increased work opportunities without increased working hours or other job responsibilities. An economic system built on the drive for profit can in such ways provide benefits of various kinds to all members of society. The freedom to gain economically in such ways is a basic right of the capitalist system. However, considerations of justice may warrant limitations on such gains, as described later.

Private Property

Profit cannot exist without the institution of private property. One cannot profit from a sale unless one owns or has control over the disposition of a product. To own private property is the right to have an extensive degree of control over something one has acquired. One must have acquired the object legitimately to have a right to own it. Legitimacy is usually defined by the laws and customs of a given society. Within our society, the right to ownership exists only if one has not violated laws of ownership and acquisition (including civil law, antitrust laws, tax laws, laws prohibiting insider trading, cheating in various ways, and so forth).*

The degree of freedom to control, use, or sell property varies with the laws of a given society. There are numerous legal constraints on ownership. To own a gun is not to have the legal or moral right to shoot people; to own a car is not to be justified in driving it at full speed on public highways; to own a house in a city is not to be able to drill for oil legally in one's backyard. Furthermore, to own may obligate one to pay taxes. Ownership has, perhaps, never implied an absolute, unqualified right to control.

The question of which legal constraints on ownership are fair or justified continues to be a matter of dispute. Some theorists have argued that ownership justifies

---

*For theoretical justifications of the right to ownership, see the works of Thomas Hobbes and John Locke.

the right of management to exercise almost complete and total power over production, employees, and company policies of all kinds within the law. Another argument is that businesses in one country cannot compete successfully on world markets unless managers have extensive powers ensuring flexibility in business practices. Workers, conversely, have argued that limits must be set on the power of management. They maintain that workers have certain moral rights to safety, privacy, freedom of expression, and due process that justify such limits. Some managers, finally, have maintained that the realities of a free and open job market are a sufficient constraint on management's power. Managers who fail to respect the well-being of employees will lose them to the competition.

Competition

Competition is natural to many aspects of human life, but is an essential defining element of a capitalist economy. Critics of economic competition see it as a mad scramble for possession of limited commodities, a way of keeping workers alienated from each other and thus more manageable. Worst of all, it is viewed as a perversion of human relationships.

Thomas Hobbes, the seventeenth-century English philosopher, traces competitiveness to the desires that are essential to human nature. For Hobbes, "The desire to acquire what is pleasurable and to avoid what is painful are the governing motivations for all human behavior." Moreover, as life progresses, our natural desires increase and we seek to satisfy them. But even as these desires are satisfied new ones appear. It is almost impossible ever to satisfy all of our desires. Competition, says Hobbes, occurs when two or more people want goods or other desirable items that cannot be shared, such as the same plot of land. This can degenerate into a "war of all against all," if no restraints are followed, Hobbes notes.

In a capitalist economy competition produces relationships of supply and demand. As demand for a given product or material increases and stockpiles are depleted, supply may fall. As the supplies of some material or product increase and it becomes more easily obtainable, its price will fall and profit may decline. It is competition for limited materials and products that drives supply and demand, prices and profits in a market economy. The extent to which such competition is good or bad, the extent to which our present economy follows regularities of supply and demand, and the extent to which the government should regulate supply and demand are important questions that cannot be addressed here. It should be clear, however, that an economy that is not heavily regulated by a strong government tends to be governed by regularities of supply and demand.

Capitalist economic systems generally allow every person the right to pursue profit, which in turn sets the stage for competition, which in turn produces efficiency, innovation, and satisfaction of desires. The extent to which any economy lacks incentives to compete economically is the extent to which it will fail to satisfy human desires and thus fail to do what an economy exists to do: produce human wealth and well-being, according to advocates of capitalism.

Competition, however, creates a number of ethical problems. Violence and other questionable conduct such as lying, stealing, or cheating will inevitably occur to some extent in a competitive environment. How to determine what sorts of conduct are acceptable in a complex market system requires evaluation of different kinds of benefits. Like comparing apples and oranges, it may be extremely difficult to determine which of such competing benefits is more desirable. If government prohibits bribery to promote genuine competition, enforcement of such law will be intrusive, meddlesome, and ultimately expensive for businesses. How much enforcement is appropriate? How far should the government go to enforce rules designed to keep competition fair and thus socially constructive and beneficial? Governments in the industrially developed countries have formulated and enforce laws against monopolies to maintain an economic climate that promotes competition and thus efficiency and innovation.

Fairness or Justice: The Ethical Component

The question of fairness or justice in business is partly related to questions of worth, taxes, labor-management relations, and the nature of fair competition. Is an NBA point guard worth $12 million a year but the president of the United States only $250,000? What constitutes just reward? That is, does the winner deserve to win, and has the winner earned the reward? When we ask whether someone deserved to win, we are usually asking whether all the rules have been followed and the player played well.

When we ask whether capitalism, the business system, is fair, however, we are asking whether the rules of business are themselves fair. The concept of fairness in use here is that central to the concept of justice. Indeed, to ask whether capitalism is fair may be to ask whether the capitalist system follows the characteristics of distributive justice. Those who maintain a conservative view of distributive justice will tend to advocate the fairness of capitalism more than those who maintain a liberal or more leftist view. Conservatives and those to their right maintain that a society that permits profit making, private property, and competition will be more distributively just than one that restricts them (more will be said about justice and these positions in Chapter 2).

All major theorists of capitalism such as Adam Smith, Ludwig von Mises, and John Kenneth Galbraith have recognized the importance of limitations or rules that govern the marketplace. Without such rules, some businesses will become dominant and take over the others, thus gaining control of the market and eliminating real competition. Even Milton Friedman, who argues that profit making is a corporation's sole moral duty, maintains that corporations should not violate the law. Adam Smith was well aware that the business climate must ensure fair competition or it will soon disappear. Laws that cover fraudulent sales practices, insider trading, labor bargaining, bidding, price gouging, and the like are designed to ensure a free and fair market place.

Laws also govern the interactions of participants in the business system to protect their rights. A consumer's right to know, the worker's right to safety, or the seller's right to be paid are all protected by business law. Such protections are justified by many considerations, but all contribute to establishment of a fair marketplace. They reveal another way in which economic success is not the only standard by which society judges business operations. Such laws are designed to ensure success within the needs of society, not success at any cost gained by any means.

Some economists have argued that one of the main virtues of a capitalistic market is that it will reward producers who correctly read the market, provide good products at a fair price, and best satisfy the customers' needs. Part of the freedom of the market is the freedom to fail, as well as to succeed. Both success and failure can be earned or undeserved. A company that makes bad business decisions, such as producing gas-guzzling cars when a gas shortage is under way, may be viewed as deserving to fail. The competing manufacturer that reads the situation correctly and produces economy cars perhaps ought to succeed. The word *ought* here implies an ethical value judgment based on a conception of justice or just dessert. It also assumes that neither manufacturer succeeded or failed because of unfair practices or illegal actions.

Some advocates of capitalism maintain that government intervention normally upsets the balance and ultimately the justice of the marketplace. An example of an unfair action that corrupted competition, according to many free market economists, was the government bailout of Chrysler Corporation. Whatever we may feel about Chrysler's recent success and profit or how many people have benefited from it, many economists say the bailout was wrong, an unethical manipulation of the free market. Chrysler had in fact spent itself to the brink of bankruptcy: one might say it had earned the right to fail. However, it was instead rewarded, rather than punished, with a government guarantee of $4 billion in loans that gave it the working capital to compete against GM and Ford, both companies that were not offered any such support. They had operated profitably but were given no rewards for having done so. Instead, they were faced with new and stiffer competition from Chrysler, which meant that their sales and profits would suffer as a result in the following years. Both GM and Ford were put at a disadvantage that was not of their own doing. Instead of allowing Chrysler to suffer for its weakness, the government rewarded it and by doing so in effect penalized GM and Ford.

Whether we agree or disagree with this analysis of the Chrysler bailout, the point is that all economists, ethicists, and participants in a capitalistic market maintain that fairness is an essential characteristic of a successful capitalistic environment. Illegal and unethical practices are objectionable because they unfairly upset the balance of economic competition. Any clear demonstration of unfairness in business practices or in the rules can be enough to lead to the passage of new laws or regulations directed to maintain the market in a state of dynamic balance.

Taken together, profit, private property, competition, and fairness are essential to the capitalist system. Inherent in each of these is an ethical element. It might seem easy to scoff at this last idea in view of the many scandals and unethical practices in business that are regularly exposed to public view. But the very outcries against such revelations indicate the gravity of the need to maintain an economic system with clear and effective rules designed to promote a dynamic and productive capitalist economy that provides broad social benefits. It is important to recognize that it is businesspeople themselves who advocate an economy that provides opportunity and rewards efficiency and innovation.

Of course, many criticisms of capitalism and its practices have been expressed. Among the most serious are those raised by Karl Marx, especially his theory that capitalism alienates workers from all that makes human life worthwhile and his claim that the economics of capitalism are self-destructive. Other criticisms have come from socialists and opponents of private property such as the French philosopher

Pierre-Joseph Proudhon, who said that all private property is theft. Most recently, environmentalists have criticized the excessive materialism and the ensuing destruction of the environment following increased production that they feel is caused by adherence to the capitalist socioeconomic model. The question many environmentalists and defenders of capitalism debate is whether capitalism is compatible with saving the environment.

Much has been written in support of and in reaction to these criticisms, which we believe is informative and provocative. However, it is not our purpose to present the debate between the pro- and anticapitalist sides. Rather, we would recommend that students or instructors who wish to explore these more philosophical debates do so—they are well worth the effort. Our purpose here has been merely to present the capitalist model and its major features to set the context for ethical decision making in the contemporary workplace. It seems clear that capitalism is the prevailing model for this activity.

CHAPTER 2

ETHICAL PRINCIPLES

2.1 THE IMPORTANCE OF ETHICAL PRINCIPLES

Ethical decision making relies on ethical principles for two main reasons. First, they express our most deeply held convictions. As such, we are said to be obligated to uphold our ethical principles. That is, if we want to act ethically and a given principle expresses one of our ethical convictions, then we have an ethical obligation to uphold that principle. Second, ethical principles play an important role in the effort to arrive at a decision about what is best in a given case. Because of their moral force, solutions that uphold them are ethically preferable. Applying these principles to a given case helps us determine what our ethical convictions demand of us.

When our ethical principles conflict with one another in a given case, we must determine which possible solution upholds the most important of our principles or, at least, sacrifices the least important of them. Although this is sometimes difficult to do, we can often find good reason to think that one solution sacrifices fewer ethical values than another or that the values sacrificed are of less importance in this case than others.

A number of ethical principles are shared widely. The following list may be helpful in the endeavor to make decisions when faced with personal ethical conflicts. The list is offered not as definitive or as a complete ethical system. Certainly other ethical principles are important, but they are not listed here. Furthermore, alternative formulations of these principles may be more helpful in some circumstances. The following formulations are offered as coherent statements of some widely and deeply held ethical values. Historically, many ethical systems do accept and apply these principles, although exceptions may exist.

You need not assume that the following ethical principles are absolutes. If they express important ethical values of yours and you are committed to trying to live by the ethical point of view, then you will find strong reason to try not to violate them. However, an ethical approach to life need not require that you never violate such principles. It demands that you do so only to uphold some other ethical principle that is more justifiably upheld in the circumstances. Ethically, you must not violate them solely for purposes of self-interest or for ethically trivial reasons. Violating such principles must have strong justification and not be done casually.

2.2 SOME ETHICAL RULES

Some broad ethical principles are sometimes referred to as *rules.* Such principles may help you apply the principle of equal consideration of interests to specific contexts. Following are some of the rules that are particularly useful in making decisions at work. They include principles with the prefix "the principle of."

The Principle of Honesty

This is the principle that you should not deceive other people. There are, of course, many ways of deceiving people, and all of them violate this principle. One form of deception is lying, which may be described as stating what you believe is false to mislead someone intentionally. A second is stating a half truth, deliberately omitting information to mislead. Another is the failure to speak at all when you know the truth and know that silence will result in someone drawing false conclusions. In addition, there are many ways of misleading people while stating the truth: body language, facial expressions, and tone of voice may be used to lead others to false conclusions. Winking and shaking your head can be used as a "tip off" and thus mislead.

It is important to note that withholding information does not always violate the principle of honesty. You can withhold information from another person, even one who has a right to it, without deceiving that person. You might frankly and openly refuse to tell the person what you know. If they do not, to your knowledge, draw false conclusions as a result, the principle of honesty may not have been violated.

The principle of honesty is important because it is the source of trust. If we are unable to trust others, communication, cooperation, and other necessary social functions become difficult, if not impossible. This is because people normally expect to be treated honestly and usually lead others to believe that they will treat them honestly, too.

The Do No Harm Principle

This principle requires that you avoid doing things that harm other people or damage their projects, efforts, or property. We have a strong duty to avoid worsening others' lives. This duty is essential for social harmony. Unless we respect the well-being of others, we cannot justifiably expect them to respect ours.

The principle of do no harm does not require us to improve the lot of others. It merely requires us to avoid harming others in direct and indirect ways. It is an idea embodied in the U.S. Constitution, the laws of most countries, and many codes of professional ethics, such as nursing, medicine, advertising, and others. The principle of do no harm is essential to the idea of legal rights and is an important basis for each of the other ethical principles described here.

The Principle of Fidelity

This rule may be summarized as the principle that you should fulfill your commitments and act faithfully. You should, first, fulfill the agreements, pledges, and promises you make. Second, you should fulfill the special obligations of the human relationships you maintain.

We make commitments in a variety of ways. Sometimes we sign our names in writing, and sometimes we orally commit ourselves to do certain things. In business and law such agreements usually take the form of a contract, and we are expected to live up to the terms contained in that contract. We also make commitments by entering certain relationships and by continuing to participate in them. When others have expectations of us, if we know what they are and allow these expectations to continue, then we are responsible to fulfill them. Such arrangements are sometimes called *implied contracts* and may be taken to be as binding as formal contracts. But whether or not we call such commitments contracts, when we make them others do expect us to keep our word and act accordingly.

Fidelity is an essential value for all human relationships and institutions, and it lies at the core of trust and cooperation. It is the tie that binds, carrying us beyond an isolated individualism and motivating us to implement the principles of honesty and harm. It can be intensely personal in nature, and violations of fidelity are often resented profoundly by others.

The requirements of the principle of fidelity vary widely in different contexts. Within our families, fidelity leads us to respect privacy and provide emotional support. Sometimes referred to as loyalty, fidelity may require trustworthiness and the willingness to put the well-being of others before our own. At work, fidelity requires that we follow the standard practices of the workplace, respecting lines of authority and established decision-making procedures. Fidelity to our subordinates, coworkers, associates, and superiors requires that when we have a problem with their performance, we first tell them the problem, offering them a chance to solve it before we take it to their superiors. It requires, moreover, that we treat our subordinates fairly and equally. Beyond this, fidelity implies that we fulfill the duties of our jobs, maintain certain levels of performance, act to support and assist, and provide timely notice when we plan to terminate employment.

There are, of course, limits to the demands of fidelity. Fidelity is not the highest ethical value, and usually does not justify violating the principle of equal consideration of interests, nor other unethical or illegal actions. To promote your employer's best interest is not viewed, for example, by legal authorities as justifying your violation of the law. Concealing pertinent product information from a customer may help make a sale while it violates the customer's right to know or even harms the customer. Such concealment is generally viewed as unethical conduct that exceeds the demands of fidelity to one's employer.

To follow the principle of fidelity is to act in ways that implement the principle of harm toward those with whom we have special relationships. But fidelity requires us to do more than simply avoid harming others. Fidelity encourages us to contribute to the lot of others in various ways appropriate to the relationships we have.

The Principle of Autonomy

An autonomous person is one with the ability to act in informed, considered, rational ways that are largely free from coercion. Autonomous people are responsible for their deeds and may be said to deserve praise or blame for them. Having access to information that is available and essential to making a good decision, such people decide on their own what is best in the circumstances. The principle of autonomy is the principle that we have a duty to allow or enable other people to act in informed, considered, rational ways.

The principle of autonomy can be violated in many ways. One may exaggerate, deceive people, omit relevant information, or use threats and other forms of coercion. Most people who violate this principle do so from the desire to ensure that others act as they want. But one can also violate the principle of autonomy by simply acting carelessly, without any particular motive. Any action on your part that somehow compromises another person's ability to obtain and use needed information, reason correctly or act freely upon an informed choice can be a violation of that person's autonomy.

We take autonomy seriously in our society. We spend more money and energy promoting this principle than perhaps any other. Our entire educational system is directed to help other people develop their autonomy. Laws that forbid deception in business, government, and other areas of life are designed to respect and facilitate autonomous actions.

The principle of autonomy is intimately and reciprocally related to other important moral principles. It is part of the basis or justification of the principle of honesty. One major reason to treat others honestly is that doing so helps them act autonomously. Deceiving people, on the other hand, deprives them of the truth and information that they need to make an informed, rational decision.

On the other hand, the principle of autonomy provides important justification for the principles of harm and honesty. These three principles are closely intertwined. One important reason not to harm others or deceive them is that doing so violates the principle of autonomy by going against their wishes or depriving them of information they need to make a rational decision. When needed information is withheld from people, they may react with resentment or anger when they discover the reality. To violate people's autonomy may thwart their goals, leading them to suffer the consequences. Violating the principle of harm may also involve violation of the principle of autonomy, as when we injure someone, causing them to be unable to act on a decision because of their injuries.

Finally, fidelity also requires a respect for the principle of autonomy, and vice versa. An important part of most human relationships is the need for each party to respect the autonomy of the other. This expectation lies at the core of most contracts and agreements. It is other peoples' autonomy we are protecting by making such formal contracts, thus freeing them to act in expectation of our promise of performance. By "putting it in writing," we offer tangible evidence as assurance that we have not deceived them, deprived them information necessary to make a rational choice, or otherwise coerced them into a deal they ordinarily would have shunned. In most cases, one cannot respect the principle of autonomy without acting in accord with the principle of fidelity.

The Principle of Confidentiality

Closely connected to the principles already presented is the principle of confidentiality. Although it is, in a sense, derived from a certain combination of them, it is worth considering separately because of its special relevance to the workplace. Indeed, confidentiality may be viewed as a uniquely professional work-related or role-based ethical principle.

This is the principle that some information should not be released to people outside certain circles. These circles or groups may be defined by the roles of the people within them, their duties, responsibilities, need to have access to certain information to perform their jobs appropriately, and their right to know the pertinent information. Respecting the principle of confidentiality protects certain people from being harmed by information falling into the wrong hands. It may prevent violations of the right to privacy.

Whether information is properly confidential in nature may be discerned by considering three factors: (1) the potential effects of releasing the information, (2) the origin of the information, and (3) the intent of those who might be affected by releasing it. If the release of certain information to someone could harm a third party in some significant way, the information is probably best treated as confidential and maintained within the appropriate circles. Consideration of the origin of information can also indicate its confidential nature. Information obtained from medical records, corporate research plans, personnel files, or private conversations that have been overheard is probably best treated as confidential. If someone has a right that certain information be kept confidential and would likely intend that it be kept confidential, this is significant reason to treat it accordingly. Consideration of any one of these three factors may provide sufficient evidence that information falls under the principle of confidentiality. The principles of harm, honesty, autonomy, lawfulness, and fidelity may offer justification for treating information as confidential.

The Principle of Lawfulness

It is important to recognize that there are four main sources of law. First and most basic are *constitutional* laws that define the political procedures of the nation, its states, and their subdivisions. Second are *legislative* laws, which are passed by formal votes of the federal and state legislatures and signed into law by the executive branches of governments. Third are *executive* or *administrative* laws, which are interpretations of the first two by the executive branch, which is charged with implementing constitutional and legislative laws. Fourth are laws formed by *judicial decisions* that interpret and apply to specific cases the constitutional, legislative, and executive laws. The principle of lawfulness recognizes the duty to follow these laws, to cooperate with those who act lawfully in implementing and enforcing them, and to seek to change them only by lawful and ethical means.

Although it is certainly true that not all laws are fair or ethically justifiable, there is still a general, ethically based duty to obey the law, especially in a largely free and broadly democratic society. In such a society, all citizens have potential influence in making the laws. If they do not find the time to exercise that influence or choose not to do so, their continued presence in that society may be interpreted as a general agreement to abide by all of its laws. The principle of fidelity may thus be one basis for the obligation to act accordingly.

Many laws are justified by their success in fulfilling the principles of harm and autonomy. Violations of the law may harm others directly or indirectly or violate their autonomy, and they are accordingly unjustifiable. Such considerations may offer a powerful justification for following many laws, even if not all of them.

If a person tries to change a law but is unsuccessful for any of a number of reasons, the person has the option of leaving the geographic area under the jurisdiction of that law. If the person chooses to stay and continues to oppose the law at the same time, the person is nonetheless bound by the principle of lawfulness to follow it. In so doing, the person is a part of what is known as the *loyal opposition.* The person is loyal in not violating the law at the same time he or she works to oppose it.

If a law is unjust and someone opposes it unsuccessfully, that person may resort to *civil disobedience,* as engaged in by many of those in the civil rights movement of the 1950s and 1960s. This approach includes public violation of the law to dramatize the need for change. Whether civil disobedience is ethically justifiable is an old and complicated issue that need not be addressed here. It should be noted, however, that civil disobedience does not include private violation of the law for the sake of one's own advantage. The citizen who quietly cheats in paying income tax because the tax seems too large is not engaged in civil disobedience. Such violation of the law is a violation of the principle of lawfulness.

Laws are often made to protect individual rights. Violations of the law may thus involve violations of individual moral or political rights. In the next section, we shall turn to consideration of the nature and importance of rights in general and a few specific rights.

2.3 RIGHTS AND DUTIES ▰▰▰▰▰▰▰▰▰▰▰▰▰▰▰▰▰▰▰▰

A *right* is a justified claim to something. That is, if someone is making a rights claim, then there is good reason for that person's claim to be recognized. If you have a legal right, then the legal system declares that you may have good reason to exercise that right. Laws are often statements of legal rights. A moral right, on the other hand, is justified within a moral system such that the moral system supports your claim to exercise your right.

Rights are options that you may or may not choose to exercise. Even if you do not exercise a right, you may still be said to have it. However, a right is not in fact recognized, respected, or realized unless the opportunity to exercise it is a viable option that you can enact without penalty. If you have a right to vote but your employer penalizes you for doing so, then your right to vote is not respected by the employer. But your failure to vote not to miss your favorite TV program reveals no limitation on your right. Missing the program may be a loss but is not a penalty imposed on you by an external source. Some cases, of course, do not admit of definite classification. Here you must evaluate them according to each situation to determine whether you are being denied your rights by an outside source.

If you have an ethical or moral right to something, then you may choose to exercise it without acting unethically. If you have a right to something, then someone else has a duty either to fulfill the right or at the least not to interfere with your effort to fulfill it. If you have a right to a tax refund, then the government has a duty to provide it. If you have a right to freedom of speech, then the government and its citizens have, at least, a duty not to interfere.

Ethical rights differ from legal rights in several ways. The former may or may not be upheld by the law. A legal right, however, is a right guaranteed by the law. Only ethical reasons and principles can justify the belief that you have a given ethical right. The mere presence of a legal right, however, is not by itself any proof that this right is ethically justified. It may exist as a result of certain political maneuvering lacks ethical justification. However, ethical reasons and principles can sometimes justify thinking that there ought to be a legal right. Many laws are partially justified by good ethical reasons or principles. For example, libel laws are justified in part by the principle of harm: to libel someone is at least to harm their reputation.

Ethical rights may be justified in part by other ethical principles or rules. The principles of harm and autonomy offer good reasons to think that government has an ethical right to require corporations to avoid false advertising. If false advertising were allowed, more people would be misled, their autonomy curtailed, and their money wasted.

Moral and ethical rights are interrelated with ethical rules. You may be said to have a right to be treated by others in accordance with the ethical rules described earlier. The justification of those rules offers good reason to think that people ought to be treated accordingly and that failing to do so is ordinarily wrong. Moreover, various ethical rights may offer good reasons to think that people should uphold certain ethical rules.

People sometimes make very forceful and insistent statements that certain people have certain ethical rights. Such statements may sound convincing, even intimidating. But you should not assume from this that they are justifiable. Such people may be upset about some matter and overstate their case. It is important not to be persuaded by the authoritative sound of the language of rights. An example might be a student claiming that because she paid her tuition for a class that she has a right to a passing grade regardless of her actual performance in the class. To claim such a right is easily done, but to justify the claim requires much more by way of support and reasoning.

One effective way to approach a statement that there is a certain right is to ask what duties are involved, who has them, and why. Such questions may well lead you to discover that such a statement is unjustified. Although it may at first sound plausible that someone has a certain right, consideration of the nature and justification of the corresponding duty may reveal cause for doubt. Would the teacher of the student in the prior example have a duty to pass every student who paid tuition? This seems a very doubtful claim, and honoring the claim would render grading itself meaningless.

Most rights imply limitations on the actions of others; some justify burdens on others. Consider the manager who asserts that she has a right to fire a subordinate. If she means that she has a legal right to do so, consideration of the law and policies of the company should resolve the question. If she means she has an ethical right to do so, consideration of the corresponding duties may help you evaluate the implications and justification of her claim. If the manager has an ethical right to fire the employee, then her superiors have an ethical duty to allow her to do so. If, however, the employee is productive, reliable, respected by his peers, and cooperates with other managers, the manager may lack an ethically justifiable reason or right to fire him. Firing him might be unfair to him and do more harm than good for the company. In such a case, upper management might well have no duty to allow him to be fired and might better transfer him to another division of the company to resolve the problem. Thus, examination of the duty associated with a supposed right may help clarify the existence of the right.

2.4 SOME IMPORTANT ETHICAL RIGHTS ▰▰▰▰▰

The number of nameable rights is very large. Some, however, are particularly useful in evaluating ethical conflicts at the workplace. The following rights and their corresponding duties express important ethical values, but they need not be thought of as absolutely inviolable. You may view them, like other ethical principles, as offering strong but not absolute ethical reason to act in certain ways.

The Right to Know

The right to know is closely connected to the duty to inform. People in certain roles and occupations have a right to know certain kinds of information. And those in certain relationships to those others sometimes have ethical duties and sometimes legal duties to provide them with the information. For example, if an auto mechanic discovers that the brakes in a customer's car are worn down, the mechanic has a duty to inform the customer, who has a right to that information.

However, although one may have a right to know something, in some circumstances another may not have a duty to inform. Rights are options, and one may have a right to know without choosing to exercise the right, without trying to find out. Although the car owner has a right to know that better cars are on the market than the one he is now driving, the mechanic does not necessarily have a duty to tell him (unless, of course, his present car is unsafe).

It is important to recognize that one can violate the duty to inform without violating the principle of honesty. Consider the mechanic who is having a busy day, frustrated by many interruptions. The mechanic might neglect to note on the work order that the wheel bearings are low on grease. Although this violates the duty to provide information, the information was not intentionally concealed and there was no deception. Of course, the mechanic may be charged with dereliction of duty or even incompetence, which are both violations of the principle of fidelity.

The Right to Privacy

This is the right to control information about yourself, or access to it. To have this right is not necessarily to exercise it. We reveal information about ourselves whenever we appear in public or engage in cooperative work. It is common knowledge that in certain situations, some information about ourselves will normally be made available to other people. Although much of this information is not clearly of a private nature, some of it may be. We may give information of a personal nature to our colleagues without clarifying its personal or private nature.

Giving private information to others does not automatically count as permission to pass it on. An evaluation of employee work performance is private information and should not be passed on by the employer without the employee's permission. The misuse of information about a person may itself amount to violation of the right to privacy.

It is possible for someone to violate your right to privacy even if you give permission to obtain the information. If you give permission under threat or coercion, the one who gathers the information may violate your right to privacy. Such permission should be given of your own free will.

Someone who has the right to know does not necessarily have the right to use any means available to obtain the information. Your employer may have the right to know who is stealing supplies from the stockroom but not have the right to invade your privacy to catch the thief by searching your car in the parking lot. The right to know is not identical to the right to obtain information by any means available.

Your right to privacy can be violated at home or at work. Beside spying on you at home, it is possible to spy on you at work. That your employer owns the workplace and is paying for your work and time does not by itself justify clandestine gathering of information about you, although this fact is often given as a justification for such actions. In some cases this reasoning may be an acceptable justification, but usually other reasons must be given in support of such invasions of privacy.

The right to privacy is important for a number of reasons. First, it can, in some circumstances, be justified by the principle of fidelity. If it is mutually understood that a work evaluation is private, fidelity requires the employer to guard the disclosure of that information. Second, if the invasion of privacy is done against your wishes, it may also violate the principle of autonomy. Third, violations of privacy often violate the principle of do no harm, causing embarrassment, loss of prestige, or even loss of a job. Moreover, the feeling that you can maintain your own privacy is essential to your attitude toward life. Violations of privacy can be seriously damaging to one's sense of pride, self-esteem, and security. Finally, the right to privacy is essential for the protection of other moral rights such as the right to think freely, to act freely, to pursue happiness, and to speak freely. Environments and societies that ignore people's privacy invariably infringe on these important moral rights.

The Right to Free Expression

This is the right to express your own opinion without being penalized for doing so. It is not, however, the right to harm your employer by speaking your mind. An employer may justifiably demote or even fire an employee who repeatedly or purposefully does significant harm to a company. The right to free expression includes the right not to be penalized merely because you said something that displeases your employer. For penalties to be justified, the effect of your statements must cause (at least be likely to cause) significant and unjustified harm to the employer.

Your intentions may also play an important role in deciding whether you have the right to express yourself freely about your employer or others. This right does not justify slander. Slander, a legal concept, is saying things that are false and damaging. It is especially unethical if your intentions are to harm the person you slander.

To become an employee is generally to agree to perform your work to a certain level of productivity. To interfere with that productivity is objectionable on two grounds. First, it violates the work contract between employer and employee. Second, it damages the employer's goals. It is for these reasons that an employer may be justified in taking reprisal against employees who make statements that irresponsibly damage their employers' interests.

It is the effects of your stated opinions, not their content alone, that may justify reprisal. Of course, divulging technical corporate secrets to outsiders may justify your being fired. It is because such secrets are essential to successful company business and because it is your duty to honor this that you should maintain them as confidential. If you violate the policies of your employer, this may warrant the employer's response on the grounds that you have proven to be no longer trustworthy. Again, claiming a right to free expression is not sufficient justification for your actions in these cases.

Suppose, however, that a company has a policy that no employees are to state their religious beliefs at work. If such a policy is not essential for the company's success, violating it may do no significant harm to the company's business. In such a case, the policy itself violates the employees' right to free expression.

Justified by the principles of harm and autonomy, the right to free expression is essential for the right to pursue happiness and other important rights. It is fundamental for any democratic society. It should not be denied at the workplace unless it is essential to furthering the legitimate purposes of the employer.

The Right to Due Process

In the workplace, this is the right of an employee to appeal a decision by management to an impartial third party with the power to correct the decision if it is wrong. The body empowered to render a decision must be composed of individuals who do not stand to gain or suffer from the decision. And appropriate procedures must be in place to guarantee that the employee receive a fair hearing.

This is a right that protects employees against the arbitrary use of managerial power. Many commercial workplaces take no steps to guarantee this right. Employees who want due process must then appeal to the civil courts. However, civil procedures are slow and cumbersome and often discourage those who have been wronged from seeking redress. As a result, many unions have established practices of arbitration that protect employees accordingly. Many governments require both government-paid employees and those of government contractors to implement appropriate procedures.

Due process at the workplace is sometimes considered an ethical right for a number of reasons. First, recognition of this right is necessary to protect all the rights and ethical rules mentioned earlier. Due process is important to the same extent as these rights or rules. Second, it is based on a combination of the principles of autonomy and harm. Employees are not the property of employers but autonomous people with the right to pursue happiness as long as it does not infringe on the similar pursuit of others. Employees can be wronged by unjust treatment. Due process gives employees the chance to seek justice when an employer has acted unfairly or arbitrarily. Third, people have a right to some influence over the decisions that affect them. They have a right to protection from arbitrary power over their lives and to work in environments in which there is a balance of certain powers. Fourth, businesses are licensed by society to provide services and products that benefit society. Businesses should and do implement the values of society, and they should not be allowed to create their own despotic subcultures.

Although some business managers have opposed the formal recognition of the right to due process in the workplace, few have advocated that their own superiors should have unlimited power over them. The principle of equal consideration of interests is one foundation of the right to due process at the workplace. Those who oppose recognition of the right to due process do so largely for their own benefit.

The Right to Safety

Employees have a right to a workplace in which reasonable precautions have been taken to protect them from bodily harm. What counts as reasonable precaution is, of course, not easy to state. However, certain general factors should be considered. Employees should be informed of known risks, encouraged to take care to avoid them, and trained in ways of doing so. But here, there are difficult questions of degree. How thoroughly employees should be educated and how much care they should take are matters requiring much consideration. These important questions must be answered in the contexts of varying workplaces and as a result of more detailed and lengthy analysis than is presently appropriate. However, that there is some basic right to safety is an important ethical consideration based firmly on principles of do no harm, autonomy, and fidelity and also on many rights.

Additionally, the right to a safe workplace protects employees from negligence on the job, that of either their employers or their fellow employees. Safety procedures that guard against injury due to negligence are reasonable measures for a company to take and for employees to expect.

2.5 JUSTICE

The concept of justice is generally used to refer to ethical issues that are not clarified by the ethical rules, rights, and duties described earlier. Justice concerns primarily the ways in which people are treated in social contexts and less commonly the ethical interactions between a small number of people. Thus, we normally refer to a society as having an unjust penal system or a corporation as having a just system of employee protections. But we would less likely refer to a thief, con artist, or a poor worker as acting unjustly.

Justice is embodied in the idea of fairness to all. We might even call justice the right to fair treatment. All versions of justice purport to implement the principles that similar cases should receive similar treatment and that equals should be treated equally. The concepts of proportionality and propriety are central to all concepts of justice. What is appropriate for one case for a certain reason may be less appropriate for another case for which the relevant reason is less applicable. Thus, punishments, for example, should be more and more severe for more and more severe crimes.

Institutions are the primary instruments of justice. Although they are often governmental, such institutions can also be corporate or educational or of some other nature. Less commonly is justice appropriately and defensibly implemented outside institutions. As noted in the section on capitalism, a notion of justice or fairness may be presupposed by an economic system. Of course, individuals within institutions are instrumental in implementing justice.

Because all people have equal value in a fundamental moral sense, everyone should be treated justly. All should be recognized as having to an equal extent the moral rights adduced previously and should be treated in accord with the ethical rules. Justice demands moral treatment of all in accord with the principle of equal consideration of interests.

There are four main kinds of justice. *Procedural justice* includes the equal chance of all people to receive a fair hearing in any disputes. Procedures designed to implement due process are attempts to implement procedural justice. This kind of justice is fundamental to a just, democratic society and is essential for a humane workplace.

Compensatory justice refers to the justice of decisions designed to compensate those who have been harmed by others. If you have been fired unjustly, slandered, or robbed, you might appeal to a court of law for compensation. The awarding of monetary damages by the court would be an attempt to implement compensatory justice. To do so, the court would attempt to determine the harm to the plaintiff and the monetary or other reparations necessary to restore you to your former state of well-being. To treat equals equally, the court would compare similar cases to determine the level of appropriate compensation.

Retributive justice refers largely to the deserving of punishment. It is based on the very old, traditional view that those who have done wrong deserve to be punished. That is, the fact that they did something wrong shows that they deserve to have something bad done to them. The justice of the situation means that the punishment should be fair and uniform. If you have done wrong and deserve to be punished, the punishment should be appropriate and similar to fair punishment for similar wrongs by others. Retributive justice is an old concept repudiated by some who argue that retribution itself cannot be rationally justified. Retribution is the belief that those who do wrong deserve to suffer simply because they did wrong. "An eye for an eye and a tooth for a tooth" expresses this idea in ancient form. Opponents argue that two wrongs cannot make a right and that harming a wrongdoer is merely another wrong deed.

Opponents of retributive justice also argue that only four considerations can justify fines and other penalties. They may be justified by the need to deter others from doing similar wrongs, to prevent a wrongdoer from doing further wrongs, to protect others from further harm the perpetrator is likely to commit, or to educate the perpetrator about the wrongness of the deed. But none of these justify retribution, and thus none of them prove that a culprit deserves to suffer, so it is argued. This viewpoint became increasingly popular during the twentieth century, but it has not by any means eliminated the concept of retributive justice from the minds of most people. There are regularly popular outcries against those believed to be criminals who succeed in evading the justice system.

Distributive justice pertains to the distribution of goods and services or benefits and burdens in a society. Here, questions of equality are the source of a fundamental dispute that has traditionally defined the main positions on the political spectrum. These positions are traditionally referred to as "left" and "right." Those on the far left include the socialists and on the moderate left the liberals. Those on the far right include the libertarians and on the moderate left, the conservatives.

Those on the far left, known as socialists, maintain that society exists to benefit its members. Because the lives of all people have equal ethical value, all people have equal ethical rights. It is government's role to guarantee equal rights for everyone. Democratic socialists believe that these rights are best protected by democratic governments that take strong steps to ensure that in the making of governmental decisions, all people and all parts of society have an equal say and equal power.

Because the lives of all people have equal ethical value, it is government's job to ensure that everyone has the basic necessities for a decent life. These include minimally decent food, clothing, shelter, health care, education, transportation and the opportunity for legal redress. In addition, socialists favor government support of institutions promoting individual fulfillment such as libraries and parks. Many favor government sponsorship of the arts and organized sports to ensure access to them by all members of society.

In the view of socialists, the greatest threat to society is the exploitation of the poor by the rich. Democratic socialists seek to limit the political power that the rich can exercise, and they tend to favor participatory democracy, when feasible. Socialists maintain that the rights to own and to make a profit are not as important as the rights of all members of society to lead a rewarding life. Therefore, government should ensure that the rich do not have too much control over the economy and political institutions of society. The government should maintain careful controls on the marketplace and ensure that economic activities benefit all in society. Such a rationale may lead government to level heavy taxes on businesses, regulate prices, and ensure that workers have power over management decisions that affect them. It may lead to government ownership of industries in transportation, health care, and public utilities.

Those on the right, known as _libertarians,_ view ethical rights as options, maintaining that only ethical rights are properly equal among all people. Everyone has an equal right to participate freely in trading and thus the marketplace. But individuals' success in the market may differ, and it should be allowed to differ. The right to own should be interpreted broadly, so that people are allowed to keep whatever profits they have legally acquired or have been given by those who have legally earned them. Moreover, government should provide people with nothing beyond what they obtain in these two ways.

Representative democracy should protect people from being harmed or enslaved and should enforce whatever rules are needed to maintain a free market economy. Libertarians hold that it is not society's responsibility to take care of those who fail in the marketplace. The plight of some does not justify taking from those who have been successful. It is not the fault of successful people that some others are unsuccessful. The wealthy should not have their possessions confiscated by government and redistributed to the poor. It may well be that individuals should help others in need, but to do so is not the role of government. Government should play a minimal role in the life of society, doing little more than maintaining a police force, a military, and a court system. But government should not redistribute goods and services. They can be most efficiently and justly distributed in society by private, profit-making capitalist enterprises.

Closer to the middle of the political spectrum are liberal and conservative views of distributive justice in a democratic society. The conservatives are located a little to the right and the liberals a little to the left of center. Liberals maintain that the equality central to the concept of justice includes both rights and, within rather moderate limits, goods and services. They hold that those who are rich are freer than those who are not and that society should strive to provide a certain minimum degree of freedom for all. They favor the existence of a free market but believe that it is best that no one be allowed to perish from extreme misfortune or poverty. Therefore, they favor redistributing to the poor some of the excess wealth of the rich. Such redistribution should, however, permit the rich to remain relatively rich. The distributions should provide a minimally decent life for the poor, including a decent minimum level of freedom and opportunity for them. They should receive what is determined by the political process of a representative democracy as necessary to make it possible for one to lead a rewarding life. In most of the developed, capitalist democracies during the late twentieth century, this model has come to include food, clothing, shelter, education, health care, transportation, and legal redress. Liberals generally hold that such goods and services should be provided to the poor to a lesser degree than socialists advocate. Like socialists, liberals tend to favor government leadership in providing certain goods and services that enrich life for all members of society. They have favored government establishment of parks, libraries, and an infrastructure including systems for sewage, drinking water, roads, and public transportation. Liberals favor less extensive government support of such institutions than do socialists.

Liberals are less interested than socialists in limiting the economic or political power of the rich. Government should, of course, take a little of the wealth of the rich to support the poor. But beyond this, the rich should be largely free to use their wealth as they choose, as long as it does not interfere with constitutional representative democracy. Moreover, the rich should be free to operate their businesses as they choose, as long as doing so does not violate basic political rights guaranteed by the constitution or the laws of a representative democracy.

The conservative view of distributive justice maintains that all of one's important moral rights can be maintained even though one is poor. According to the conservative position, the wisdom of the ages shows that poverty does not diminish human dignity. It is not the job of government to ensure that all have sufficient means to live. Rather, the job of government is to maintain the openness and freedom of the marketplace, preventing monopolies from taking over and protecting individuals from being harmed by others. To do this, government should maintain a few public institutions such as a system of law enforcement and courts and perhaps public education. Conservatives have come to accept government responsibility for tending to parks and maintaining the infrastructure consisting of roads, sewage, and drinking water, though they favor less government support of such institutions than do liberals.

The job of government is not, for conservatives, to ensure the survival of the poor or homeless. However, recognizing that starvation is not a pretty sight, conservatives have increasingly tended to grant that society may, if it can afford to do so, choose to provide a "social safety net" for unfortunate people who have lost their jobs. This should be a small and temporary allotment of very basic goods and services, provided to help them while they reestablish their places in the market, thus searching to sell their labor or products. The social safety net is a smaller allocation of goods and services to the poor than that advocated by liberals, and its purpose is temporary assistance.

Conservatives generally believe, however, that the proper workings of the market economy will provide enough wealth and benefits so that the poor will be provided for. It is the belief of many conservatives that allowing the market to work with little governmental intervention is the best way to create the wealth and institutions necessary to provide for the poor. Moreover, the creation of private wealth is likely to create more jobs and opportunities for the poor to better their condition without governmental assistance. Conservatives believe that it is the free market system that can most effectively better the lot of the poor, rather than an intrusive governmental redistribution of wealth. This belief separates conservatives from socialists and some liberals who hold that only governmental intervention can ensure a just distribution of the benefits and burdens in a society.

Conservatives and liberals both maintain that society should provide for all of its citizens an equal opportunity to enter the marketplace of labor, goods, and services. Opportunities should be provided for all citizens to obtain education, and job positions in the government should be nondiscriminatory. However, conservatives differ from liberals in their view of those who do not, for whatever reason, take advantage of educational opportunities and do not gain satisfactory qualifications for a job. Conservatives and libertarians hold that this is no fault of society and that government should take no further steps to benefit such unfortunate people. Assistance to such people should be left to the goodwill of individual citizens and private organizations devoted to providing charity.

Liberals and socialists maintain that equal treatment of citizens implies that government provide extra opportunities for those who do not take full advantage of educational opportunities to establish employment qualifications. Moreover, liberals and socialists argue that nondiscriminatory government hiring policies do not go far enough to eliminate racial, gender, and other kinds of discrimination. All organizations should take positive steps, or affirmative action, to encourage applications from and seek out job candidates from certain minority groups that have traditionally been discriminated against in society. This requires, in the view of some liberals, that employers hire minority members who are at first unqualified and train them on the job.

Liberals and socialists on the left differ from conservatives and libertarians on the right regarding many other issues. In the main, these differences are based on disagreement over the question of whether poverty and lack of social and economic opportunity unduly restrict one's rights, liberty, and dignity. Those on the right argue that history proves that a life of poverty does not necessarily diminish one's rights, human liberty, or dignity. Those on the left argue that social realities prove that one's rights, liberty, and dignity are significantly diminished in a life of poverty.

2.6 SELF-INTEREST ▰▰▰▰▰▰▰▰▰▰▰▰▰▰▰▰▰

Self-interest is not often thought of as an ethical principle. An ethical principle must be consistent with the principle of equal consideration of interests, which imposes a limitation on self-interest. ECI demands that you pursue your self-interest only to the extent that doing so does not treat the interests of others as less important than your own. However, even granting that limitation, self-interest in some contexts may have some ethical justification.

There are reasons to believe that each of us has an ethical duty to take care of ourselves. First, to fail to do so is to act in a way that impoverishes a small part of society: yourself. Second, a society in which people ignore their duties to themselves would soon disintegrate and its members die off. Third is the fact that most people are happiest, most well adjusted emotionally, when they take care of themselves. Fourth is the argument from tradition: values that have stood the test of time must have some real importance.

One approach to the argument from tradition is known as the *principle of conservatism.* This is the principle, embodied in the law, that one should not interfere with an ongoing practice unless there is clearly good reason to do so. The mere fact that an ongoing practice may be doubted, or may have disadvantages, is not sufficient to warrant interference with it. The burden of proof is on the critic to establish that altering the practice will do more good than following it. It is not the responsibility of those who favor the practice to establish its worth. The mere fact that it has persisted to become tradition does count as one significant reason to think that it has some value. This is often called "passing the test of time." Those who want to alter the practice can be justified in doing so only if they can provide sufficient reason to believe that the alteration truly does more good than harm.

One traditional, ongoing practice of human beings is to teach their young to take care of themselves and to pursue their own self-interest. Moreover, responsibilities to oneself are embodied in the teachings of many of the great religions of the world, thus expressing the considered judgment of humankind over the ages. These offer significant reason to think that the pursuit of self-interest, as long as it does not contradict ECI or religious law, is an ethical, fit, and proper endeavor for human beings.

2.7 THE NETWORK OF ETHICAL VALUE ▰▰▰▰▰▰▰▰▰▰▰

It is important to recognize that the ethical principles presented here are all interrelated in meaning, their import for our lives, and their justifications. The system of ideas here may be thought of as a network, each intersection of lines an ethical principle connected to the others directly or indirectly. Ethical values are not neat, isolated units that can be adopted or ignored at will. Rather, each one has extensive implications for others. To develop an understanding of one principle will often lead to further insights regarding others.

What is common to each of the principles, and which may be thought of as the material constituting the strands of the network, is the principle of equal consideration of interests. That is, one who follows the other principles carefully will generally be acting in a way that treats others' interests and well-being as having as much importance as one's own. If this principle may be thought of as defining the ethical point of view, each of the other principles assists us in applying that point of view to concrete, specific situations.

It is not clearly helpful or accurate to represent ethical principles as related in an hierarchical manner, as if some were fundamentally or universally more important than others. It is true that ECI is implemented by the other principles and is, in one sense, more general and fundamental than they. But ECI is not, practically speaking, more important. That is, in specific situations, ethical people do not usually find that ECI conflicts with other principles or that these principles should yield to it. Rather, conflicts of ethical value are usually defined by reference to the other principles. The ethical resolution of such conflicts ordinarily implements ECI in the best way possible.

The network of value is perhaps best viewed as having considerable flexibility. The flexibility applies to the relationship of the various principles in different concrete situations. In some situations, two or more principles may be closely intertwined such that a given decision may violate several at once. In others, a decision may violate only one. In one situation, the best decision may be one that upholds one principle but violates another; in another situation, the best decision may do the exact opposite.

Taken together, the principles in the network of ethical value comprise what is sometimes referred to as an *ethical worldview.* They offer counsel on a wide variety of life's problems. Most who advocate and live by some of these values also accept others. At the basis of every society is broad agreement among many people on most of these values. The list of ethical principles discussed here is certainly not exhaustive. However, any expansion of this list would likely include the addition of principles and concepts that partially include and are partially defined and justified by reference to those described earlier.

The ethical principles presented here need not be viewed as beyond question. None of them need be viewed as absolute or unexceptionable. They have limitations and might perhaps be justifiably reformulated for various purposes. The importance of these principles must be distinguished from their exceptions. An ethical principle may be extremely important even though there are some ethically justifiable exceptions.

Members of the same society tend to agree broadly on the content of major ethical principles such as those presented here. Most disagreement arises in the application of such principles to specific situations. Indeed, some of the most important and challenging work in ethics occurs in the application of these ethical principles to specific, concrete, day-to-day situations. This is the challenge of personal ethical problems. The next chapter shows you how to use the RESOLVEDD strategy of decision making to help you work through some difficult ethical problems. It develops a sample analysis of the case outlined in Chapter 1 that applies some of the ethical principles explained here.

CHAPTER 3

THE RESOLVEDD STRATEGY OF ETHICAL DECISION MAKING

The RESOLVEDD strategy is a way of thinking through a personal ethical problem to arrive at the best decision you can. The best decision is one that upholds your most important values to the greatest extent possible in the situation at hand or is most consistent with your ethical character, all things considered. Because your ethical values are some of your most important values, the best decision is usually an ethical decision, one that upholds these values to the greatest extent possible.

An ethical decision is one that upholds the principle of equal consideration of interests; that is, it treats the interests or well-being of others as being at least important as your own. If an ethical decision violates any ethical principles, it does so only to uphold or avoid violating some other ethical principles that are more important in the case. One important goal in ethical decision making, then, is to determine which ethical principles or values are the most important in the case at hand.

An ethical decision is normally a decision on which you would be willing to stake your reputation. It is one that you think is right on the basis of ethical principles that you try to follow and that you believe others should follow. It is a decision that you believe is right for people of good character to make in such cases. Ethical decisions are usually decisions in which you can take pride, knowing that you have tried in earnest to apply your ethical principles honestly. You can then know you have done your best to be a good person in the situation at hand. You can identify with the decision you have made, believing it is a decision that is suitable for a good person. Thus, your conscience is at peace, and you are ready to enact the decision and live with its consequences.

At times none of this is easy, none of the available options are clearly ethical, and the consequences of the apparently best solution are unfortunate. Herein lies the challenge of ethical decision making. There are, at times, no simple solutions. The RESOLVEDD strategy does not remove the difficulties of ethical decision making. However, it can help you clarify those difficulties, examine them from several perspectives, work through them systematically, and make a well-informed choice. The strategy arranges the things that we normally think about when making ethical decisions and that many ethicists have accepted as important, in a way that makes the thought process clearer and easier to apply.

3.1 AN OVERVIEW OF THE RESOLVEDD STRATEGY

The RESOLVEDD strategy can, but need not, be represented as a series of steps that one follows in a certain order to develop one's analysis and decision. In fact, one's thinking need not follow these steps in exactly this order. It is normal, in thinking about a case, for one's mind to jump back and forth among the different parts of a RESOLVEDD analysis and for new ideas in one part to generate new ideas in another. The main parts of an analysis are described here as steps for the sake of the initial presentation of the strategy and in a useful order for written analyses. But your thinking about the case need not follow exactly this order.

Step 1—R: *Review* the history, background, and details of the case.

Step 2—E$_1$: State the main *ethical problem or conflict* present in the case.

Step 3—S: List the main possible *solutions* to the case.

Step 4—O: State the important and probable *outcomes* or consequences of each main solution.

Step 5—L: Describe the *likely impact* of each main solution on people's lives.

Step 6—V: Explain the *values* upheld and those violated by each main solution.

Step 7—E$_2$: *Evaluate* each main solution and its outcomes, likely impact, and the values upheld and violated by it. Compare the possible solutions with each other and weigh them.

Step 8—D$_1$: *Decide* which solution is the best; state it, clarify its details, and justify it.

Step 9—D$_2$: *Defend* the decision against objections to its main weaknesses.

Step 1 is the very beginning, which should involve a careful review of the context and background of the case, its origin, and important details. You might look at this as getting the facts and context of the case straight.

Step 2 should be the initial thoughts or estimate of the ethical problem(s) or conflict(s) that the case presents. The understanding gained in this initial estimation may later change as you develop the analysis. These two steps lay the groundwork for the following considerations.

In step 3, you state briefly the main possible solutions to the case. Before stating them, you may start with a list of many possible solutions and then group them together, simplifying and narrowing down the list to a more manageable size. Here you are trying to consider any possible solutions that occur to you; more may occur to you later on, and many may drop out of consideration quickly. The initial multitude of variations of these main solutions may become important later, in the seventh and eighth steps. The next three steps will develop a sustained analysis of the main solutions as they are formulated in the third step.

In step 4, you identify the main, most likely, and important possible outcomes or consequences of each main solution. Consider the question "If I choose solution A, then the following things might happen" and then go on to list them. Answers to this question will ordinarily lead you to address considerations that constitute part of the fifth step. The outcomes, as opposed to likely impacts in step 5, are the general consequences of your choice. These could include what might happen to the company, society, or a competitor.

Step 5 is the beginning of your formal analysis. It involves the especially important job of considering and stating the likely impact of each main solution on people's lives. Will a solution likely hurt or help people, and in what ways? Here you are trying to determine how individuals are affected by the general consequences you have identified in step 4. What you might ask is a question such as "If the company is sued [an outcome from step 4], how will the workers, managers, my supervisor, or I be affected?" The fourth and fifth steps provide information that is essential to the analysis of the case you will develop in later steps. These fourth and fifth steps suggest to you, rather naturally, the ethical principles upheld and violated by each main solution.

In step 6, you explain and clarify the main values or ethical principles at issue in each main solution. The task here is to clarify which values or principles are upheld and which are violated by each main solution. Simply naming these principles is not enough. It is essential in this step to explain just how and why each main solution violates or upholds these principles.

Until this point, you have taken stock of the case, noted the main options, listed the important outcomes and likely impact of each, and clarified the values at stake. Now, in step 7 it is time to evaluate the main solutions, compare and contrast them, weigh them to determine which are better, which worse, and why. In this seventh step, you make value judgments about the seriousness of the violations of values and the importance of upholding the values described in step 6. That is, you state your own views on the nature and significance of the ethical issues and present your reasons for holding these views. You explain why, for example, some outcomes are more likely to occur than others, some likely impacts of main solutions are more significant than others. This seventh step may well be the longest, most involved, and difficult of all. It requires you to take a stand on various issues, formulate reasons for your opinions, and question and evaluate them. As you work through the seventh step, you will eliminate some main solutions from further consideration. You will formulate arguments to justify your value judgments and conclusions. Your work in this step will be drawing to a close when you have eliminated all but one main solution.

It is important to realize that you may think of new possible solutions as you pursue this seventh step. You may discover that you had neglected an option early on and that it offers considerable promise. It is important to maintain an open mind to the possibility that the solutions you identified earlier in the analysis do not exhaust all of the possibilities. In-depth analysis in this seventh step may well lead you to a new possible solution that turns out to be the best decision.

The point at which it becomes clear that you favor a particular main solution is the point at which step 8 begins. This is the step in which you develop and support your decision. A number of things need to be done in this step. First, refine your preferred main solution and describe the specific course of action you think is best. The details of your decision are important. You cannot determine whether the decision will really work unless you consider these details carefully. Second, explain why you favor the main solution that you do and why it is ethically preferable to the others. Third, examine the specific course of action you have decided on and show why you think it will work and why it accomplishes the goals you seek in the case. Fourth, justify your view that this specific decision is the best one in the case, taking all important values, outcomes, and other considerations into account. This may require repeating and summarizing some of your analysis from steps 4 to 7, especially from step 7. Do not be afraid to do so; repetition, if done well, can clarify and strengthen your analysis for others.

The ninth step is to defend your decision against the main objections to it. Whether or not you have formulated the perfect decision, someone else may be inclined to cite one or more significant weaknesses of your decision. Your job in this step is to state and explain these weaknesses and defend your decision against them. That is, you need to provide an answer to those objections to show why your decision is still the best one, despite the alleged disadvantages or weaknesses of it. You are anticipating your critics and answering them before they can raise their objections, which usually indicates that you have done a thorough and balanced job of analyzing the situation.

Some of the parts of the RESOLVEDD strategy may be covered in a slightly different order than discussed here. Some of the steps can appropriately be mixed in with the others. Thus, one may do some evaluations immediately after listing some outcomes or likely impacts of main solutions, and after clarifying the values upheld and violated by main solutions. But it would be jumping the gun to cover step 8, one's decision, before stating, analyzing, and evaluating the main solutions, their outcomes, likely impacts, and value implications. There are important reasons that the parts of the analysis are suggested in the order they are. But this order need not be viewed as rigid and unalterable.

3.2 APPLYING THE **RESOLVEDD** STRATEGY TO THE CASE OF YOUR SUBORDINATE

A description of the Case of Your Subordinate is found on page 1. What follows is an analysis of this case as developed by some of our students. Although far more can be said about the case than is included in this analysis, it does illustrate an application of the RESOLVEDD strategy. The steps of this analysis are in the following order:

Review of the case

Ethical problem in the case

Solutions 1 and 2

Outcomes 1 (outcomes of solution 1)

Likely impact 1 (likely impact of solution 1)

Values 1 (values upheld and violated by solution 1)

Outcomes 2 (outcomes of solution 2)

Likely impact 2 (likely impact of solution 2)

Values 2 (values upheld and violated by solution 2)

Evaluation

Decision

Defense

A RESOLVEDD Analysis of the Case of Your Subordinate

REVIEW   This case arises from pressure from my boss to take unusual steps with an employee who is a poor worker. However, it seems clear that although Grindel's work is below par, it is not substandard and offers no grounds for firing him. He is not really doing anything wrong, although he may be one of the worst employees I have. Management has decided to force me to aid in their attempt to get Grindel out.

In the ranks of management, managers are not supposed to make decisions for their subordinates. My boss should not be giving me orders about what to do, nor should he expect that I will necessarily carry out this suggestion. But he might very well expect that, and I must be very sensitive to this suggestion and not accidentally offend my boss by flagrantly ignoring it.

ETHICAL PROBLEM OR ISSUE   It is clear that my problem is not Grindel! My problem is caused by my boss's suggestion that I do something that is rather sneaky and mean and not entirely ethical. That is, my problem is how to react given the suggestion of my boss in light of the fact that what I do may unfairly violate the principle of harm where Grindel is concerned.

According to the case description, my boss only suggested a solution to the case but did not order it. I am under no clear obligation to do exactly as he suggested. But does the principle of fidelity mean that I owe it to my employer to try, within the limits of acting ethically and legally, to find a way to raise productivity? And I will have to find a way to communicate to my boss effectively the rationale for my decision. That decision will need to be one that my boss agrees with and that is best for the company.

Thus, it seems my main problem concerns whether to violate the principle of do no harm to uphold the principle of fidelity, or vice versa. Other values will surely be involved as well.

SOLUTIONS   I could (1) do as my boss suggests, rotating Grindel among the most undesirable jobs, or (2) resist my boss's suggestion and handle the case in my own particular way. If I choose this second approach, I have several options. These include my continuing to counsel Grindel, giving him time off to attend training sessions, or persuading the union to put pressure on him.

OUTCOMES 1   If I do as my boss suggests and rotate Grindel among the most un-desirable jobs and shifts on the production floor, my boss might be pleased that I am following his suggestion. On the other hand, Grindel might figure out what is going on (after all, Grindel is only lazy, not stupid!) and begin to seek avenues to stop it. If he took the case to the union, he might win a grievance on the grounds that my strat-egy is harassment. If he didn't figure it out, he might quit.

LIKELY IMPACT 1   Following my boss's suggestion would likely make Grindel quite upset, even to the point of him quitting or filing a grievance. This in turn could backfire on me if Grindel was successful in gaining his fellow workers' attention and sympathy. The whole thing could turn into a nasty, demoralizing, and efficiency-reducing labor-management conflict. Grindel could be harmed, I could be harmed, and the workers and the company could be harmed by the conflict.

VALUES 1   Doing as my boss suggests would be a way of upholding the principle of fidelity toward my boss and the company. I would be respecting the chain of com-mand and taking steps to address a personnel problem and increase efficiency. It could also alleviate some of the harm to the company the boss sees Grindel causing by his poor performance.

This first solution would violate the principle of autonomy toward Grindel. Merely shifting him around to the worst jobs without informing him of my motives would not put him in a position to face the challenge squarely and make the best, most rational decision. The shifting might cause him to become confused and de-moralized, therefore inhibiting him from thinking positively in terms of the real choice he in fact has. Although I would be happy if he were to quit, he does have a right to understand that he need not do so and a right to consider seriously the possi-bility that he might shape up instead. Not giving him the chance to confront the boss's allegations violates his right to know and perhaps even due process.

Similarly, this strategy would violate the principle of honesty toward Grindel by hiding my true motives from him. It would violate the principle of fidelity toward Grindel, as I would be acting in a way which is hardly faithful to him, and not clearly in his best interests. Rather than helping production to run smoothly, this solution would have the single purpose of sabotaging one person and making his life miserable by ma-nipulating him. It would, thus, violate the principle of do no harm toward Grindel.

OUTCOMES 2   If, on the other hand, I implement the second solution, ignoring my boss's suggestion and handling the case in my own way, my boss may view me as stubborn and inflexible. He may just get someone else to do what he wants. But if not, I can handle the situation more fairly.

LIKELY IMPACT 2   Ignoring the suggestion could lead to my receiving a poor job performance review (JPR). But if my own method of handling the case is effec-tive, this might redeem me in the eyes of my boss. Grindel will likely not suffer as much if I handle the situation well. Of course, Grindel will still be harmed and might take it out on me personally. If the other workers see it his way, I could have to deal with a lot of unpleasantness every day at work.

VALUES 2   Ignoring my boss's suggestion might be viewed as violating the principle of fidelity toward my boss and employer by failing to respond appropriately to the lines of authority that I was hired and obligated by my job to uphold. However, there is some room for debate here, because my boss only made a suggestion, and it is not completely clear that I am expected to follow it as if it were an order. If the boss holds me responsible, though, I can be harmed by losing his support and a bad JPR.

This solution upholds the principle of do no harm if I can handle it so that Grindel feels he has been treated fairly. The principles of autonomy, right to know, right to due process, honesty, and fidelity will all be upheld with respect to Grindel. My handling of the situation, if done well, will not violate these values as solution 1 did but rather uphold them by treating Grindel fairly, with respect and in a way that preserves his autonomy. I will not be harmed, either, by the negative reactions of Grindel and his fellow workers.

EVALUATION   The main problem with the second solution, ignoring my boss's suggestion, is that doing so would jeopardize my boss's high opinion of me and thus my JPR. It is not a significant violation of the principle of fidelity, as my boss merely suggested but did not order me. However, there is reason to doubt that any effort I make to solve the problem on my own would likely be successful. This makes all the values upheld by solution 2 "iffy." That is, if I cannot find such an equitable solution, I will end up violating them anyway. Given Grindel's personality and my total failure to get him to cooperate so far, it seems unlikely that I will have much luck in my efforts to reform him. This second solution would be personally risky, although not ethically problematic. But what good is a decent solution if you can't actually pull it off?

The first solution, following my boss's suggestion, on the other hand, has a number of advantages. It might be best for Grindel if it succeeds in motivating him to shape up or ship out. However, knowing him and perceiving the meanness of such an approach, I do not believe it likely to have such a salutary effect on Grindel. It would be treating Grindel in an underhanded and inconsiderate way, failing to respect his need to know why he is being treated in this way, violating his autonomy and right to know. Such treatment for any employee is clearly not ethical and cannot be justified by the fact that Grindel himself has not acted cooperatively or fairly. In reality, two wrongs do not make a right. That is, it is not right to counter one wrong with another. Moreover, as noted, this solution has the potential to create significant practical management problems that waste large amounts of time and energy, reduce morale and productivity, and are detrimental to my career. Following this choice seems to violate the principle of do no harm in many ways: for Grindel, for me, for the other workers, and for the company itself. This option is the worst choice on all important grounds.

The main problem with the second solution, disregarding my boss's suggestion and addressing the problem myself, is its threat to my career and the harm that would follow. There must be some personally less threatening ways to deal with my boss's casual suggestions and thus relieve me of their burden. Once I have done so, I would be free to address the problem with Grindel in some more creative and less ethically and practically objectionable ways. Here I might be able to respect Grindel's autonomy, right to know, avoid harming him and be truthful toward him, at the same time maintaining the fidelity I owe to my boss.

DECISION   My decision would be first to have a serious, in-depth, heart-to-heart talk with my boss, explaining to him in a very diplomatic and nonoffensive way all the disadvantages of shifting Grindel around. I would do so in a way making it obvious that upper management would likely look askance on that solution. I would then proceed to explain the nature of the ethically acceptable alternative measures available and outline my plan to pursue them. This strategy would show him that I have taken his suggestions seriously, value his opinions, and am bent on addressing the problem in a way that is best for the company overall. I would stress strongly the principle of do no harm as it pertains to the company but also emphasize the need to respect Grindel's rights.

I think that once he realizes the significance of the union-management conflict that could result from shifting Grindel around, my boss may well be willing to admit that we should just turn our backs on Grindel. If so, he might then suggest that I simply drop all concern with Grindel. But I think I can take steps that have not yet been tried with Grindel, may have some hope of success, and would cost the company very little.

DEFENSE   One problem with my approach is the possibility that my boss might be bullheaded about it all and insist that I defer to his greater experience and authority. If I were to do so, I would be setting myself up for a very bad JPR in the future and reduce my chances for advancement. However, if my boss turned out to be as autocratic as this, no solutions would be good for me personally. Clearly, then, my best approach is to use every means at my disposal to convince him of the benefits of my handling the case in the best manner I know how.

A second problem is that no matter what I do, Grindel may not respond. If this happened, then I'd have failed, my boss could hold me responsible for the failure, and Grindel would still be hurting the company. However, this can be said to be true of every situation in which we try to influence others' behavior. They simply may become irrational and not listen. If this happened with Grindel, I think my boss would be open-minded enough to see that it wasn't my fault. After all, he had failed with Grindel, too. Even if I am held responsible, I can take some comfort in the fact that I did the best I could and treated Grindel fairly. His unfair or irrational reactions are not under my control. All I can do is my best. However, I don't think Grindel will get totally irrational, nor do I think my boss would miss the fact that I cannot simply order Grindel to act rationally.

3.3 UNKNOWN FACTS

A description of a personal ethical problem may make no mention of certain factual information that is relevant to your decision and that you might be aware of if you were actually in similar circumstances. The description of the Case of Your Subordinate offers no clear information about the context of or the nuances of the suggestion made to you by your boss. Yet, in actuality, you would have such information, and it would play an important role in your decision. However, when such information is not stated in the case description, you should assume it is not known and develop your analysis and decision with as little reference to it as possible.

It is important to recognize that most decisions are made in the presence of significant factual uncertainty. There are *always* important facts that decision makers simply do not have. All decisions are based on a degree of speculation. If we waited until we knew every possible fact, we would never be able to decide or to act. The author of the present analysis speculates on the question of how likely it is, if your boss's suggestion were implemented, that Grindel would cause trouble once he figured out what was being done to him. There is also speculation on how likely you could persuade your boss of your point of view. Decision making in ethics, as in all fields, requires you to respond thoughtfully to the different possibilities regarding unknown facts. Of course, a miscalculation on such questions can lead you to make a decision with disastrous consequences. It is part of the art of effective decision making to learn how to address and work with such uncertainties.

3.4 LACKING TIME

It takes considerable time and concentration to develop an analysis of a personal ethical problem. Yet, such a conflict may occur in a complex situation demanding a quick decision. How can the RESOLVEDD strategy be of help in such high-pressured situations?

Of course, sometimes you cannot work out a complete RESOLVEDD analysis. In such cases, you have no choice but to rely on various habits of thought that you have developed in advance. Such habits can be developed by practicing the RESOLVEDD strategy on cases such as those presented in this book. Practice may help you become more familiar with ethical principles such as those presented in Chapter 2. You may become better able to detect situations in which these principles play important parts. You may be able to determine immediately that a certain possible decision upholds or violates a certain important principle. Such quick grasp of the important ethical factors in a conflict is sometimes described as *intuition* or *insight*. Practice in using the RESOLVEDD strategy can help you develop and sharpen your intuitive abilities.

As you develop facility with the RESOLVEDD strategy, you may need less and less time to develop an ethical analysis. You may find that you need less time to cover the more routine steps of the strategy. This, in turn, may give you relatively more time to consider the most trying issues of a conflict.

Practice in applying the strategy may help you establish value judgments that are useful for further ethical conflicts and help you reduce the time needed to analyze them. If, in some future case, you face an issue that you addressed earlier, the approach you took before may be applied again, thus saving you further time. On the other hand, a mistake you made earlier may well have taught you a lesson that is of central importance in some future conflict. With increased practice, each new ethical conflict will become less novel and need less time for analysis.

The pressures of time undeniably can increase the likelihood of making unsatisfactory decisions. It is certainly best to use as much time as possible to address and analyze personal ethical problems. Through practicing the RESOLVEDD strategy, you may progress from making thoughtful analyses to making better decisions in less time. The more practice you have, the more the whole process becomes "second nature" to you. When you reach this point, you may find that ethical analysis, though perhaps no easier in the sense of cutting through the difficult issues and conflicts, can be done more quickly. Do not, however, sacrifice the quality of your thought process for speed. A good analysis is more important than a quick one. Where the situation demands a quick solution, having practiced and followed the RESOLVEDD strategy will be an asset, even if you must react quickly.

3.5 A CHECKLIST

Review

____ What are the particularly important relevant details of the case?

____ How did the situation come about?

____ Is something wrong? What? Why?

____ Is anyone at fault? Who? Why?

____ Is there likely to be disagreement over the case from people related differently to it? Why? What are the different perspectives that people may have on the case?

____What information would you like to have that is missing and that you must decide without having?

Ethical Problem

____ What options do *you* have in the situation?

____ Why is it difficult to make a decision in the case?

____ Initially, what do you think is the main ethical conflict in the case?

____ What main points will you need to consider in making the decision?

Solutions

____ Group the options into a small, manageable number of main solutions. Remember that you may end up deciding to do something that is not exactly like any of the solutions with which you began.

Outcomes

____ What are the significant possible consequences of each main solution?

Likely Impact

____ In what ways is each main solution (you might implement) likely to affect people's lives by hurting or helping them?

Values

____ What important ethical principles are upheld by each main solution? How?

____ What important ethical principles are violated by each main solution? How?

____ Have you explained how each main ethical principle is violated or upheld by each main solution?

Evaluation

____ Are some consequences of some possible solutions more important than others? Why?

____ Does one solution uphold or violate certain values in more or less important ways than another? Why?

____ Why is one possible solution better or worse than another?

____ If all main solutions are unsatisfactory, have you searched for other possibilities? Have you considered that new unthought-of possibilities may be hidden in your main solutions and that you might find a variation of one that is satisfactory?

Decision

____ Exactly how will you carry out your decision? Explain the details.

____ Just why is this decision the best, all things considered? Explain.

Defense

____ What are the main weaknesses of your decision? Why might someone object to your decision?

____ If these weaknesses have not been stated and addressed earlier, do so here.

____ What are the best answers to these weaknesses? Why do you still think your decision is the best? Explain.

CHAPTER 4

ASPECTS OF THE RESOLVEDD STRATEGY IN DEPTH

The prior chapter offers an initial presentation of the RESOLVEDD strategy and an analysis of the Case of Your Subordinate. The present chapter addresses, in more depth, some of the questions one confronts in developing a RESOLVEDD analysis.

4.1 WHEN IS AN ETHICAL PRINCIPLE UPHELD BY A GIVEN SOLUTION?

The mere fact that a given solution does not violate an ethical principle does not show that the solution upholds the principle. Consider, in the Case of Your Subordinate, the solution of ignoring your boss's suggestion and moving ahead to handle the case as you prefer. Such an approach clearly does not violate the principle of confidentiality. But neither does it uphold that principle in any significant way. Rather, that principle is not relevant to the decision of whether to follow that solution. That is, the principle of confidentiality does not offer a reason either to follow or not to follow that solution. It is best, then, simply not to mention that principle in step 6, the values portion of your analysis.

Consider, however, whether the principle of do no harm is relevant to (giving evidence for or against) the solution of refusing to follow your boss's suggestion and doing something else instead. Because following the suggestion may do harm to Grindel, refusing to do so may avoid doing harm to Grindel and so may be said to uphold the principle of do no harm. Just why is this so?

Following your boss's suggestion is an important possible solution to the case. The fact that doing so violates a particular ethical principle and not doing so does not is an important ethical consideration that must be considered by any reasonable person deciding what to do. We express the importance of the fact that not following your boss's suggestion does not violate the principle of do no harm by saying that it upholds that principle. To summarize: to say an ethical principle is upheld is to say that the fact that it is not violated is an important ethical consideration for one trying to decide what to do in the case. In other words, if a principle is upheld, you could use the principle as a reason in support or defense of your decision.

The following is a condition that must be present for a given ethical principle or value to be upheld by a given solution: For a solution to uphold a value, there must be some other solution to the problem at hand that would violate that value. If a given value is not violated by any possible solution to a personal ethical conflict, then the value need not be mentioned in your analysis. Such a value is not relevant to any decision regarding the conflict and should probably not play any significant role in your analysis. There may be a possible main solution that violates a certain ethical principle but that is extremely unattractive for various reasons. In such a case, you would have no significant reason to state that the alternative solutions uphold this ethical principle. In such a case, this principle is largely immaterial to the decision at hand.

Consider a possible (but outrageous) solution to the Case of Your Subordinate. You could simply hire a hit man to take out Grindel! Such a solution would violate the principle of do no harm! But this hardly justifies your citing as an advantage of the other possible solutions that they uphold the principle of do no harm. Making such a point is generally unnecessary because this is such an extremely bad solution.

Citing this application of the principle of do no harm as an advantage of other solutions is unnecessary for one who is trying to live by the ethical point of view. A second condition for a value to be upheld, then, is that the alternative solution that violates it is worth being considered by an ethical person. These two requirements for a value to be upheld can be combined into one:

> For a solution to uphold a value, there must be some other solution that would violate the value. The other solution must be worth serious consideration by an ethical person.

Another way of thinking about whether your solution upholds a principle or value is to ask, "Could I use the principle or value in question to support or to justify my decision?" A principle or value is upheld by a solution if you could use that principle or value to argue in favor of your solution. If the principle or value offers good reason for another person to accept your solution as the correct one, then it is upheld by your solution. Remember, to uphold a principle or value means that the principle or value can be used as a reason to support your particular solution.

On the other hand, a principle or value violated or sacrificed by your solution means that it could be used as a reason to reject your solution. If your solution violates a principle or value, then that principle or value could be used by someone who disagrees with your solution as a good reason for saying your solution is not justified. Such a principle or value, then, could be cited as justification for others to see your solution as incorrect and as a reason to ask for another alternative solution. The question here is "Could someone use the principle or value in question to reject or criticize my solution?" If the answer is yes, then the principle or value is violated to some extent by your solution.

4.2 A SOLUTION CAN UPHOLD AND VIOLATE THE SAME ETHICAL PRINCIPLE

It is important to recognize that a given solution to a personal ethical conflict can both uphold a given ethical principle and violate it at the same time. This apparent paradox is possible because of the broad and general nature of major ethical principles. As you may have noted already in the Case of Your Subordinate, failing to carry out your boss's suggestion may both uphold and violate the principle of do no harm. It may uphold the principle in avoiding doing harm to Grindel and violate it in causing more trouble for you, your boss, and the company.

These considerations help clarify the importance of explaining, in step 6, the values section, just how a main solution violates a given ethical principle. The important point is not that an ethical principle is violated by a solution. It is the specific way in which it is violated that you must consider in the evaluation of the solution. The mere fact that an ethical principle is violated by a solution does not prove the solution is ethically wrong. Awareness of such violation is merely awareness of one reason to think the solution is wrong. But other, more important reasons may explain why it is the best solution given the circumstances. These can only be understood and evaluated by examining the specific way in which the ethical principle is violated.

Ethical principles are general in nature. Each concrete situation pertains to a given principle in a slightly different manner, depending on the particulars of the situation. Ethical decision making requires that one look very carefully into those particulars and understand each situation as a unique instance of the relevant ethical principles. Each instance will embody the ethical value of a principle in its own unique way, and to a greater or lesser extent. Your decision must emerge from careful consideration of the ethical values uniquely present in the various alternative main solutions.

This is not to say that ethical principles are relative or subjective. The principles and values are not changed by considering each unique application of them on a case-by-case basis. The same principle may apply differently to different situations. So each situation requires a reevaluation of the relevance of ethical values. The most influential ethicists of our age, such as W. D. Ross, have long recognized this point. Relativism, on the other hand, typically involves the view that the very principles and values themselves are changed or re-created by the unique aspects of each situation. Relativists tend to maintain that each person, each time, each place, and each new element of a situation create the need to revise or manufacture new ethical principles or values. Such a view offers little hope for the prospect of learning from our ethical successes and mistakes.

The more common view of ethicists is that our principles and values commonly remain the same although they affect our decision making in different ways in various situations. This view does not imply that every person has new principles for each situation encountered. Rather, we should analyze and evaluate each new situation and our relevant principles before we understand fully how or whether they apply to that situation. As time and experience pass, we learn more about our principles and how they relate to the world and thus develop moral wisdom.

4.3 WHO SHOULD I CONSIDER WHEN DOING THE O AND L STAGES?

Often students have asked of the RESOLVEDD strategy, "Who am I supposed to consider when I look at outcomes and the likely impact on people's lives?" Usually this question arises as a result of looking either too narrowly or too broadly at the O and L sections. That is, sometimes we tend to focus on only ourselves, people we are directly concerned about, and perhaps the company itself. Other times we look at absolutely everyone when we consider moral decisions. Both approaches can lead us into errors. Either we leave important consequences and individuals out of our analysis, or we get bogged down trying to imagine how our decisions affect people beyond those who are actually involved and important to our analysis. But how do we answer the question of just who needs to be considered?

Perhaps a good way of responding is to apply a concept that has become very widely accepted in the literature of business ethics. The concept is that of a *stakeholder analysis*. A *stakeholder* is anyone who has a stake, a reasonable interest, in the actions of a company or individual employed by the company. Stakeholders are people who can be affected by a company's actions or by the choices made by individuals working for the company. Stakeholders have reason to care about how the company or its employees act because those actions affect the stakeholders in some way. Therefore, we can say that, when doing the O and L sections of the RESOLVEDD strategy, a good rule to follow would be to consider the outcomes and likely impacts of our choices on all stakeholders.

Exactly who might qualify as a stakeholder can vary from case to case, depending on the circumstances and effects of the chosen action. In general, stakeholder analyses are meant to broaden the scope of people to consider when making an ethical decision in business beyond the shareholders, employees, and consumers of the company's product. Many corporate actions affect the public, whether the public holds stock in the company, works for the company, or purchases the company's product. To limit our consideration of consequences to these three groups no longer seems acceptable to many ethicists, though at one time it may have.

Some choices may affect only a few people in a small department of the company, whereas others may affect a large number of people outside the company. An example of the first sort might be the choice of whether to require all the machine shop personnel to take their lunch at the same time, even though the employees want to be free to choose their own lunch schedules. This decision will not affect production or the operation of other areas in the plant. Although it is conceivable that other employees might be affected if the lunchroom became too crowded, we will assume this isn't a problem, nor is there a problem with the shop being closed for the half-hour lunch period. Here the only people who have a stake in the decision are those managers and workers in the machine shop, so the stakeholders are limited to these two groups.

An example of the second type would be a decision to ignore current warnings about safe levels of a toxic pollutant discharged into the local river and to stick to the now outmoded guidelines the EPA applies to the company. Here the company's choice affects everyone living downriver from the plant because they could be adversely affected by the toxic waste, especially if drinking water is drawn from the river. Negative publicity might also cause a drop in sales, so that consumers are turned off and decide to buy a different brand. Layoffs might follow if sales drop too low, so the workers are affected. Shareholders may lose money as the stock drops because of the loss of sales and negative publicity. Managers, especially those who chose to ignore the warnings, may be fired or transferred. Even politicians who failed to enact stricter controls could be affected if the public votes them out of office. Thus, this decision affects a large number and wide range of people, all of whom are stakeholders with an interest in the company's choice of pollution controls. It would be wrong and a violation of the principle of equal consideration of interests to ignore their interests if you were the manager making this decision.

Stakeholders, then, include every person who has some interest in or reason to care about an ethical decision made in the workplace. The ECI principle justifies taking all stakeholders into account when solving personal ethical problems. Anyone affected by your choice should be considered. Stakeholder analysis broadens our perspective so that we include everyone who is justifiably said to have reason to care about a corporation's or individual's actions. You should not limit your analysis to those who have a monetary interest in a company or decision (shareholders, for example) because many of the effects of ethical decisions may not be monetary effects. Health effects, psychological effects, and effects on family relations are often important whether or not those affected have a monetary interest in the company.

Thus, a workable answer to the question "Who should I consider in the O and L sections of the RESOLVEDD strategy?" is "Consider the stakeholders." If you take the stakeholders into account, you will be considering the effects of your actions on the people who are actually affected by your choices. Be careful not to limit your scope to employees and stockholders or to broaden your scope too much by considering absolutely everyone in your analysis. Not everyone is going to be affected by every choice you make, but many choices you make will affect even those who have no monetary interests in the decision. Asking whether a person has a stake in the choice you are making can help ensure that your analysis will be a reasonable one.

4.4 UNDERSTANDING THE EVALUATION STAGE

It is important to understand the difference between describing the outcomes, likely impacts, and values upheld and violated by the main solutions and the evaluation of these three. The evaluation is not simply a summary or a combination of the other steps. It involves some fundamentally different kinds of thinking and is essential for arriving at a well-considered decision.

Statements that are characteristically within the solutions, outcomes, likely impact, and values steps are all objective and descriptive. These are statements presenting the basic, ethically relevant facts of the case. They are not statements asserting that you believe that something is really right or wrong, good or bad, or has a particular degree of value.

To state as a main solution "I could do as my boss suggested" is to say that this is a possibility. It is not to state a value judgment regarding how good or bad the solution is. It does not assert that your own values give any reason to think that the solution is good or bad.

To state an outcome or likely impact of a solution is to describe one or more possible consequences of it. It is not to state how important the outcome or likely impact is or whether it is desirable or undesirable. Additionally, it is not to suggest that or how or why you weighed alternative principles or values to decide which were most important to you. To indicate your opinions on such matters is to evaluate them and belongs in the evaluation stage of your analysis.

This distinction between the application of concepts and your own value judgments is pertinent to the sixth step regarding values upheld and violated by a possible main solution. Consider the following: "For me to tell Grindel that my boss has suggested we get rough with him would be to violate the principle of confidentiality by disclosing a private conversation with my boss." This statement merely asserts that the solution violates an ethical principle. But it does not present your evaluation of this violation. It does not indicate, for example, whether in your view it is ethically insignificant in comparison with other ethical principles at stake in the case. The statement does not indicate whether you think the harm done is serious or how serious it is. It does not indicate whether the harm done by such a talk with Grindel is as serious as the harm that would result from dropping the issue altogether. Nor does it indicate whether you think the violation of confidentiality is ethically justifiable. In other words, it does not explain how you weigh or rank the values in importance. These are matters of evaluation that need to be stated and supported with reasons and that constitute the seventh step of the RESOLVEDD strategy.

To evaluate, then, is to present your opinion of what is right, wrong, good, bad, important, insignificant, or ethically justifiable or unjustifiable. It is to begin to develop your own point of view after you have clarified the facts and principles that are relevant to the case. It requires that you make value judgments and then present and weigh the reasoning, evidence, or considerations that support those judgments. The result of evaluating is that you eliminate certain options from being worthy of consideration and rank the others in order of preference in light of your point of view. The evaluation stage exhibits your reasoning to others and to yourself so that they and you can see clearly how and why you have reached the decision that you have. It is in a sense "thinking out loud" so that others can understand your thought process as well as your decision.

4.5 AVOIDING MORAL AND ETHICAL ARITHMETIC

In the process of evaluating, you may be tempted to take a shortcut that is best viewed as unhelpful and misleading. This is the temptation to count the values upheld and the values violated by each main solution and then decide that the solution that upholds the largest number of values or violates the smallest number of values, or upholds the greatest number of net values, is the best. Such a procedure may be described as "moral arithmetic" and is seriously misleading.

To count the number of values upheld and the number violated assumes that each value upheld or violated is of equal importance in both ethical and other relevant ways. This, however, is not always the case. Within a certain situation, for example, a violation of confidentiality may not be as ethically significant as a violation of some other value. Indeed, it is possible that a certain solution could violate one ethical principle while another violates many and that the first solution is still the worse of the two.

4.6 MORAL AND OTHER IDEALS ARE RARELY HELPFUL

The discussion of ethical values in Chapter 2 omits consideration of a whole group of important ethical principles described by the philosopher Bernard Gert as ideals. An *ideal* is a moral principle that encourages one to seek to improve the world by striving to reduce the presence of evil. Ideals express high values to which some people aspire yet that they recognize as difficult to realize fully. For every moral or ethical rule, there is a corresponding ideal. For the moral rule that one should not harm people (the principle of do no harm), there is a moral ideal that you should try to help people (the principle of beneficence) and thus act to relieve pain. For the moral rule that you should not break your promises (the principle of fidelity), there is the moral ideal that you should act to help people resist breaking their promises. For the moral rule that you should not deceive people (the principle of honesty), there is the ideal that you should act to prevent deception. In general, rules require you to avoid doing harm, whereas ideals encourage you to try to perform good deeds.

Advocates of an ideal take it very seriously, often to the point of believing that it embodies the very highest value to which a human being can aspire. They may even view it as essential to a meaningful life. Ideals may be important sources of personal motivation.

Ideals may be thought of as defining a moral maximum, whereas rules define a moral minimum. To violate a moral rule is to do something that is, ordinarily, wrong. However, you cannot, properly speaking, violate a moral ideal. You may fail to live up to its strong demands and thus fall short of a high and worthy goal. But in doing so, you do not necessarily act wrongly. You can sometimes avoid opportunities to help others without actually hurting them. From an ethical perspective, it is bad to hurt people but not always bad not to help them. To this extent, you are ethically required to follow moral rules, but not moral ideals.

Although moral ideals may express our highest moral aspirations, they do not necessarily express more important values than moral rules. It may be worse to violate a moral rule than a moral ideal. If it is wrong to murder people, then it may not be justifiable to do so to make the world a better place by eliminating a gangster. Acting to uphold a moral ideal ordinarily does not negate the wrong done by violating a moral rule. In the end, a deed that violates a moral rule usually does more harm than the amount of good resulting from the extent to which the deed upholds a moral ideal.

There are, of course, other kinds of ideals, such as religious or political ideals. Some of the relationships among these other ideals and corresponding religious, political, and other principles are similar to the relationship among moral ideals and moral rules mentioned here. Consider the Christian ideal expressed in the golden rule (do unto others as you would want them to do unto you). Although a Christian believes that people should strive to follow the golden rule, Christians generally do not view the failure to do so as seriously wrong as murder or stealing (both forbidden by the Ten Commandments).

The case of Lieutenant Colonel Oliver North, the White House attaché for President Reagan, may serve as a case in point. North lied, deceived government officials, and violated government policies and laws in a number of ways during the Iran-*contra* affair in the mid-1980s. Throughout the Senate hearings and his trials, he tried to establish that he did these things to serve the best interests of the United States. He tried to dramatize to the nation that he acted on noble motives and had strived to live up to the highest ideals of patriotism. However, few were persuaded by his appeals, and he was, initially, duly convicted on the grounds that the ideal of patriotism was no justification or excuse for violating the law and the moral rules that it implements. Few were persuaded that attempts to live up to an important ideal negate, override, or compensate for violations of the law and moral rules and other ethical principles. (North's later acquittals on most charges were based more on legal technicalities than on the view that his patriotism should excuse him.)

There is no denying that religious, moral, or political ideals may be more important for some individuals than their moral or other corresponding rules. However, those who violate moral rules to uphold their cherished ideals often seem to do so out of a zealous and partly blind enthusiasm that ends in violating the rights and values of other individuals. Those who seek to uphold an ideal, and in doing so violate a moral rule, are sometimes referred to as fanatics. A *fanatic* is a person who does what is ethically wrong to uphold some ideal or cause in a way that is not ethically justifiable.

Although your ideals may be important to you, this should not reduce your respect for others' interests. The principle of equal consideration of interests (ECI), that we should not treat the interests of others as less important than our own, is of real significance in this context. It is one important basis of all the moral rules, rights, and principles discussed in Chapter 2. Although this is not the place to defend this principle, its importance is clear from the fact that it has been largely supported for the past two centuries, in different formulations, by many of the most important thinkers and writers on ethics. No coherent basis has been offered for the view that ideals provide sound justification for violating ECI.

Consideration of moral and other ideals has been deferred until now because they are rarely helpful in resolving personal ethical problems. People differ greatly in their interpretations of such ideals and in their views of proper implementation. Such diversity does not prove any one version of these ideals to be mistaken, or less important than another. However, the ideals should be treated with caution and not assumed, without careful consideration, to justify violation of other moral or ethical principles or ECI. Insofar as rules, rights, and other values effectively implement ECI, these should be taken very seriously before they are sacrificed to do what appears to follow some moral, religious, political, or other ideal.

There is one kind of situation in which you may find it helpful to consider the extent to which a given decision fulfills one of your important ideals. This may occur when you find that all other ethical considerations in the case are distributed evenly over, and thus evenly balanced for and against, two or more alternatives. That is, no other compelling reason exists to do one thing or another, one of your important ideals favors a certain decision, and the application of that ideal in the circumstances is consistent with ECI; then that ideal may offer you good reason to make that decision accordingly.

4.7 CONSCIENCE AND INTUITIONS

Most people who are concerned to try to act ethically have a conscience. To have a conscience is to have the inclination to feel guilty for doing something wrong. A conscience may play an important role in your life, for it is something you probably want to avoid violating. Your conscience may at times serve you as an indicator of right and wrong. That is, you may sometimes find that you have a clear intuition, feeling, or sense that a certain course of action would be wrong, although you do not yet clearly, consciously know exactly why. Such intuitions are useful, as they help us make up our minds in situations when there is too little time and a split-second decision is needed. However, it is important not to rely too heavily on our conscience or intuitions, for they are not foolproof. Sometimes the content of intuitions and "pangs of conscience" are not clear or coherent, and other times such hunches are misleading.

Conscience may be thought of as a red flag, a warning sign that perhaps something is not quite right. You should take the warning flag seriously as an indicator that you should carefully consider the situation in which it was raised. However, you must still decide for yourself what to do and whether conscience truly does indicate the best course of action. Further reflection and analysis may be necessary to determine just what your conscience really does indicate and whether the verdict of your conscience or intuitions is correct.

The best way to make a decision is to consider all sides of the case; weigh the import of all possible outcomes, likely impacts on peoples lives, and relevant values; and choose in light of these. The RESOLVEDD strategy will help you conduct that investigation on your own, given adequate time. Use of the strategy will likely help you develop your ability to analyze personal ethical problems and may thus strengthen your powers of intuition and conscience.

It is important, however, that you do not cite your conscience or intuitions as reasons that favor or oppose a given decision. Conscience and intuitions are vague notions whose apparent content needs to be questioned, analyzed, and evaluated as much as any other voice to which we listen. Moreover, reliance on your personal intuitions can lead you into relativism and subjectivism, both of which are questionable sources of moral justification. Use of the RESOLVEDD strategy should sharpen your powers of intuition and conscience and teach you not to be guided blindly by them.

4.8 DEFENDING YOUR DECISION

The last step in your analysis is to state the most significant weakness of your decision and defend that decision against it. The specific nature of a main weakness depends on the particulars of the case. Perhaps you have been overly optimistic in thinking your decision will resolve a certain practical problem in the case. Or perhaps your decision violates some important principle for a less important reason. You may have underrated the odds that a given outcome would materialize or that a person's life would be affected in a certain way. On the other hand, you may have overlooked in your analysis to this point another solution that might appear to have more advantages than your stated decision.

If you identify an objection to your decision that is so serious that you cannot defend your decision adequately, you may need to go back and reconsider some other possible options. You may need to reformulate your decision and possibly even your evaluations. Your task is not finished until you have established, to the best of your ability, that your decision is the best one possible in the case, all things considered.

This final step in the analysis is in many ways the most trying. Once you have formulated your decision and defended it, you may feel rather confident about it and perhaps even proud that you have come this far and done so well. You may find it emotionally difficult to switch to the role of critic of your own work. Before taking on the task of critic, it may be helpful to let some time lapse after completing the eighth step. Time may help you gain some perspective on your work, admit you are human and have limitations, and grant that others normally and reasonably disagree about many things we do and believe. Such disagreements need not reflect negatively on us. Rather, they may offer valuable insights and suggest to us ways to broaden and strengthen our own thinking.

Another helpful strategy is to tell someone else about the case and ask for suggestions. Others may offer reflections and perspectives that you had not thought of. Their ideas may raise questions that you should address. They may help you maintain a more objective stance toward the case and your analysis. The effort to carry out this ninth step may help you learn important lessons about yourself, your thinking, and the case at hand.

4.9 TIPS AND REMINDERS FOR WRITING A CASE ANALYSIS

When you are writing a paper covering the points of the RESOLVEDD strategy, keep in mind several points:

1. In the review of the case, be sure to state important and relevant facts that contribute to the case's ethical problem without merely paraphrasing the case. Do not try merely to paraphrase the case study. Clarify the significant facts that the reader needs to know to understand how and why the conflict occurs.

2. In the estimation of the ethical conflict stage, be sure to state the main principles in conflict to clarify the problem's ethical aspects. State at least one main value or principle upheld and one violated by each main solution. For example, it is worth asking, "Should I uphold fidelity to my boss by carrying out the suggestion, or should I find some other course of action that does not violate Grindel's rights and interests?" It is less helpful to say simply, "Should I carry out the suggestion or not?" Recognizing some of the ethical considerations here will be useful later when you work on the values stage.

3. For the solutions stage, it is important to understand clearly in your own mind that you are merely listing the main options available without all of the possible details. Given variations of detail, each main solution could be divided into perhaps a dozen specific possible solutions. This would be too many to address specifically in a few pages of writing. So the main solutions are just broad, general ones that should be identified to help you begin your analysis. However, it is crucial to remember that you may well end up with a decision that is different from any of the main solutions stated in this third step. In the evaluation stage you should bring in important details that may be used to create later, in the decision stage, a specific resolution to the problem that is best overall.

4. For the outcomes and likely impact stages, be sure to be complete and specific. Take account of all parties affected, including yourself and such parties as the general public and other companies and organizations. You may wish to follow the practice of doing a stakeholder analysis as a way of including all relevant parties in your analysis.

5. For the values stage, be sure to explain how and why each principle is upheld or violated by each main solution. A list of such values or principles without clarification of how they are upheld and violated is of little or no value. It does not contribute to understanding the nature of the ethical problem at issue or of the advantages and disadvantages of the many different options available.

6. In the evaluation stage, be specific and detailed about your reasoning. How and why you decide which values are most important must be explained fully. State and defend your own personal views on the importance of both the principles you have clarified in the values stage and the consequences clarified in the outcomes and likely impact stages. It is essential to explain to the reader the reasoning that you used to arrive at your own personal viewpoint of which are the most important values and consequences in the case.

7. In the decision stage, summarize the values and other reasons that support your decision. You need not repeat most of what you have stated in the evaluation stage, but you may need to summarize it briefly and perhaps state some reasons that were not stated directly there. Explain in detail how your decision will be carried out. These details are essential to determine how workable and realistic your decision is.

8. In the defense stage, you should state the main weakness of your decision and then provide a defense against that weakness. In doing so, you are answering an objection to your decision, not simply repeating your main justification. To do this, you should first, in your own mind, put yourself in a critic's position and focus on the weaknesses of your own analysis. Then reply or answer the objections to show why they are not strong enough to cause you to abandon your decision. If truly no objections are possible, say so. However, such a finding usually occurs because of your own lack of imagination rather than because you have formulated the perfect decision!

Keeping these tips in mind while you think through your analysis and write it out will help avoid some common faults. Such weaknesses usually result from a lack of detail in the thinking and writing. Effective use of the RESOLVEDD strategy requires attention to conceptual detail and to the reasoning you develop. It may help for you to think of your job as that of providing an argument for your position to someone who will initially disagree with the conclusion. By clarifying certain crucial points listed by the RESOLVEDD strategy, you are presenting the reader with enough reasons to change his or her mind and accept your conclusion. Attention to the details of your position and your thinking will help you develop a position that is best regardless of how strong of a critic you might face.

CHAPTER 5

TWO ANALYSES OF PERSONAL ETHICAL PROBLEMS

Following are two personal ethical problems accompanied by analyses illustrating applications of the RESOLVEDD strategy. In reviewing them, you may find it helpful to identify in the analyses the exact locations of each of the RESOLVEDD points.

5.1 SIN OF OMISSION

You live in a city of about fifty thousand people and sell real estate for a local realtor. Your client, Ms. Bayotic, is single, middle-aged, and a new arrival in town. She is looking for a small house suitable for her to live in alone. You have shown her several houses in her price range, one of which appeals to her because it is attractive, well cared for, and located in a pleasant neighborhood.

Despite its appeal, the house does, to her mind, have a drawback. It is older than she had wanted, and she is concerned about buying an older home. She is afraid of hidden problems in its plumbing, electrical service, or structure that might cost her more in the next few years than she can afford.

You have a strong desire to make a sale. The market has been depressed for several months now, and you have not sold a house in more than a month. Your bills have been mounting, and pressure is rising from home to "bring home the bacon."

In mulling over the problem, one thought occurs to you that might offer a solution. You could suggest to Ms. Bayotic that she call the city hall and request one of their housing inspectors to check out the house and give her a report. Although the city does not advertise this service, it does allow its inspectors to inspect houses for individuals for a fee of $60. The unbiased opinion of an impartial third party might well allay Ms. Bayotic's worries and secure the sale.

The problem with such an approach is that the city inspectors are famous for the trivial nature of many of their observations. When you bought your own house last year and had it inspected, they turned in a long list of very petty violations of city code. They listed the lack of a handrail in the stairway to the basement, the lack of an overhead light in a hallway, and the lack of an exhaust fan in a bathroom. Although they did not require you to remedy such infractions, you are afraid that a similar list might well scare off Ms. Bayotic for false reasons.

You have no clear legal obligation to suggest that Ms. Bayotic look into this city service or to inform her that such a service is available. The National Association of Realtors Code of Ethics does not specifically state that one should inform one's clients of such a service. Article 9 of the code states, "The Realtor shall avoid exaggeration, misrepresentation, or concealment of pertinent facts relating to the property or the transaction. The Realtor shall not, however, be obligated to discover latent defects in the property or to advise on matters outside the scope of his real estate license." But it does not require realtors to inform clients of all possible ways in which they may obtain opinions about a house. Article 9 is broadly interpreted to refer to the condition of a house itself and services that the realtor offers the client. Local realtors interpret it to refer to facts about the house rather than facts about what one may do to gather further information about a house. Indeed, it is standard practice among local realtors to avoid mentioning the inspection service to clients and to sell houses that have not been inspected.

It is clear at this point that to sell the house, you will have to promote it strongly. You believe honestly that the house is in "good condition." But you now wonder whether you have any ethical obligation to inform Ms. Bayotic about the city inspection service. What should you do? Analyze the case until it is RESOLVEDD.

5.2 AN ANALYSIS OF "SIN OF OMISSION"

This is a case that is clearly irrelevant to the law and on the fringe of professional ethics. Ethics does play a role in the case, however, for I must consider Ms. Bayotic's well-being as well as my own. To satisfy my own needs should not be my only goal as a salesperson. In making a sale, I also have a responsibility to help my client.

The mere fact that other real estate salespersons do not inform their clients of such information does not make it right. Established practice may be a reason to do something but should not be the only reason. In my analysis, I will need to consider very carefully the relevance of the principle of equal consideration of interests, as I do have an obligation to treat my client in a manner in which I would be willing to be treated myself.

The principal ethical issue in the case is whether I owe it to Ms. Bayotic to give her this information. The proper relationship between real estate salespersons and their clients is what I need to consider.

The case has three main solutions. First, I could do as my competitors do and not tell Ms. Bayotic about the city inspection service. Second, I could inform her of the service and take the accompanying risks. Third, I could have the inspection done without her knowledge and decide what to do with the information later.

If I choose the first solution and do not inform her of the service, she may or may not buy the house, and it is not clear at this point which is more likely. If I try to promote the house strongly, this solution might work or scare her off. On the other hand, if she finds out about the service from someone else, she may wonder why I did not tell her, and she may lose trust in me.

The only reason I would choose to withhold the information from Ms. Bayotic would be to facilitate the sale of the house. Doing so would be motivated partly by the desire to benefit myself. But because I think the house is a good buy for her, withholding the information may benefit her. So withholding would uphold egoistic value and also her well-being.

My withholding this information from Ms. Bayotic would be a violation of the principles of autonomy and fidelity. I would be deliberately withholding information that could enhance her ability to make a more informed choice. I would be making this decision partly for egoistic reasons and partly to promote her best interests. But I would be withholding information that she could use, and I would be doing so without her consent. Therefore, it could be argued that withholding would be a breach of trust.

If, on the other hand, I choose the second solution and tell Ms. Bayotic about the service, she may or may not decide to use it. And it is not at all clear whether her using it would or would not have a strong influence on her decision. If I explain to her the pettiness of much of the inspectors' reports, this might neutralize some of her concern. My telling her might also increase her respect for and trust in me. Whether or not she buys the house, informing her could in turn lead her to recommend future clients to me.

Telling her would uphold the principles of autonomy and fidelity, by enhancing her ability to make a well-informed decision and by giving her this relevant and possibly helpful information. It would not violate any important ethical values, although it might, arguably, be a sacrifice of my own egoistic value.

If I choose the third solution and order the inspection done without telling her, I may have to pay for it myself. On the other hand, I might be able to persuade the owner of the house, or even Ms. Bayotic, to pay for it. If the inspection came out well, it might be a significant selling point for Ms. Bayotic. If it did not come out well, I could drop it or decide to show it to Ms. Bayotic anyway. Several options would still be open.

Ordering the inspection without telling Ms. Bayotic might uphold my own egoistic advantage and might aid Ms. Bayotic if it helped her realize what a good house it really is. It might thus uphold the principles of autonomy and fidelity by helping her decide and by my doing my best for her. The fact that it might cost me some money shows that I am willing to take a risk for her benefit.

Ordering the inspection on my own violates the principles of autonomy and fidelity in different ways. First, ordering the inspection is done primarily for my benefit. She would not be in a position to make any decision about the inspection report unless I decide to tell her about it. So this solution might well be motivated primarily by my own desires and secondarily by concern for her well-being. And I would be acting faithfully to her only after I had determined that telling her would benefit me.

The third solution, ordering the inspection myself, has serious disadvantages. First, doing so places my own well-being above that of Ms. Bayotic. There would be no good reason to inform her of the inspection unless it turned out well. If it turned out poorly and I informed her I had it done, it would simply scare her off. Second, if I told her about the inspection after it was done, she might wonder why I had not told her first. She might think that I was simply pulling strings behind her back and lose trust in me. This solution would violate the principles of autonomy and fidelity and risk my reputation. It is best avoided.

Evaluation of the outcomes and likely impact of the first two solutions provide little help in resolving the case. The consequences of neither decision are more likely to occur than those of the other. The ethical values at stake in the case are somewhat more helpful, for the failure to inform Ms. Bayotic would violate the principles of autonomy and fidelity. However, I do not think that either principle is seriously violated by withholding the information. Salespersons are not expected to inform their clients of every possible avenue they might pursue to arrive at a decision. Both the lack of clarity on the matter in the Realtors' Code of Ethics and the standard practice of other salespeople support this point. Moreover, the city does not advertise the presence of the service and seems unconcerned to encourage people to use it.

The facts that I very much need to make a sale and Ms. Bayotic needs a house are important aspects of this case. My own desire to make the sale together with my knowledge of her needs incline me to be extremely positive about the house. But this worries me. I might be too positive and apply too much pressure and thereby scare her off. I need to be aware of the limitations of my own ability to influence her and the possibility that the "hard sell" might backfire. The point here is that even my own egoistic needs do not clearly show that withholding the information is the most effective way to make the sale or to benefit myself or her.

On balance, then, only two considerations reveal a significant difference between the two best choices of telling or not telling: the principles of autonomy and fidelity. Withholding the information is a violation (even if only a weak one) of these ethical principles, and informing her of the inspection service is not. These two principles are the single outstanding considerations in the case, and they convince me that I should indeed tell her about the city inspection service.

I would tell her about the service and explain to her carefully the nature of the report that would result. In doing so, I would not try to scare her but simply try to be straightforward, working toward the single goal of helping her as best I can. That way, she can decide for herself whether she wants to use the service. And if she makes the decision herself, she is less likely to be shocked by the results of the inspection.

My decision to tell her does have a number of advantages. First, my telling her is more clearly ethical than not telling her. Furthermore, in doing so, there are advantages for me personally. For one thing, I will have no doubts that I am doing my best for her. For another, this can only help my reputation in the long run. Finally, even if she does not choose to buy the house, she may come to trust me and develop a sense of loyalty to me, and she may ask me to show her other houses. I may end up selling her a house after all, even if not this one.

The only serious disadvantage of this decision is the possibility that she may, as a result, buy neither this house nor another one from me. But the disadvantage of this decision does not point to a corresponding advantage of the alternate decisions. For there is no good reason to think that withholding the information or ordering the inspection myself would be any more likely to secure the sale.

5.3 AN OFFER TO SPY

You had been working for almost three months for a discount dry goods store stocking shelves when the manager called you in one morning for a talk. She wanted to recommend you for a job that would nearly double your salary for at least the next three months. Tired of the boring work of stocking shelves and the low wages, you expressed immediate interest. Your boss responded by adding that the job would be confidential and that all discussions about it including the required interview must be kept confidential. You were surprised but still interested. She then handed you the address of the local corporate offices for the franchise and told you to drive there at once for the interview.

When you arrived and presented yourself to the receptionist, you were promptly led in to the executive office of the local vice president of the franchise. She was cordial and began by asking you about yourself and your ambitions. You explained that as a third-year university student, you liked the opportunities offered by big business and were planning to obtain a beginning management traineeship after graduation. As you talked and she interacted with you, you realized that the two of you seemed to communicate well. Then she made you the offer.

The vice president explained that they needed a trusted employee to help management find the thieves who had been stealing electronic equipment from the stores for almost six months. The company had tried several strategies that had failed, including notifying the police, hiring a detective firm, and interviewing employees. Now they were going to install hidden cameras in the employee lunchrooms and lounges of the stores and on the loading docks for twenty-four-hour surveillance.

The vice president was asking you because you were a relatively new employee with few ties to the others, were not a union member, and are ambitious. You are, in her view, the perfect person for this clandestine job. The problem is that in your view you are not. Having just recently completed a course in ethics, you are concerned about violations of privacy that will probably result from the hidden cameras. Indeed, it is clear to you that such hidden cameras are highly objectionable even though they in fact violate no laws.

Now you must decide whether to take the job that you want and need. So you thanked the vice president and told her you would think about it and give her your answer in forty-eight hours. That is the time you have to see this inner conflict of yours RESOLVEDD.

5.4 AN ANALYSIS OF "AN OFFER TO SPY"

Hidden cameras are objectionable for a number of reasons. First, because they are hidden, they may pick up employee conversations and actions that are potentially embarrassing or immoral, even if not illegal. Second, there are many questions about what may be done with the information gained. Will it sit in a file or on a tape somewhere, waiting to be used by some manager at a time and place of choice? What counts as the right time, and who will decide? Who will safeguard access to this information, and how well? All of these need careful attention for hidden cameras to avoid violating important ethical values. Third, because the cameras are hidden and unknown by employees and others, their very presence violates the right to privacy. Fourth, employees cannot exercise any right to due process regarding the information gained by the cameras until their presence is exposed. One cannot complain about such information unless one knows it exists. Fifth, hidden cameras involve deception if those under surveillance believe they are not being observed. To this extent, such cameras would violate the trust of employees and others.

My ethical problem arises from the fact that I am now convinced that the cameras should not be installed without proper safeguards and without employee knowledge of them. Because I have already complained to the vice president, I have nowhere further to go but outside the store management, possibly blowing the whistle and exposing the cameras to the employees or the public. However, I am personally afraid of stirring up a controversy, making enemies and possibly damaging my reputation in the local area. Ethically, my problem is whether I have a stronger duty to my employer to prevent further harm or to protect the privacy of other employees and the trust of the rest of society.

My main options in the case are to (1) ignore the whole issue and quietly install the cameras, telling no one; (2) refuse to complete the installation of the cameras; or (3) complain to other workers, the union, and perhaps the newspapers.

If I quietly install the cameras, the culprits may be caught, or the hidden cameras may be discovered by other workers and an uproar may occur. On the other hand, I might not be implicated by the whole thing and may never hear of it again.

If I quietly install the cameras, the private or personal lives of employees and others may be compromised. Whatever happens, it may eventually come out that I was the one who installed the cameras, and my reputation may be damaged accordingly.

Quietly installing the cameras would uphold the principle of fidelity to my employer by following the initial agreement I made. It would also uphold the principle of confidentiality by keeping the job-related information under control. It would protect the autonomy of the store and franchise managers, their rights to try to catch the culprits, and the company's right to own and control its property. It would, moreover, also uphold the principle of harm by not interfering in the company's effort to protect itself.

Quietly installing the cameras would violate the principles of fidelity and harm toward my fellow workers because I would be an accomplice to management's violation of their rights to privacy, due process, and to be treated nondeceptively.

The second solution, refusing to install the cameras but not complaining further, might keep me out of trouble. If my boss thinks well of me, she would probably not fire me from my present job of stocking shelves. Furthermore, she might be afraid that if she did, I might expose the hidden cameras to the newspapers. The likely impact of such a solution would be that the cameras would likely be installed by someone else, and my name would escape connection with them.

The second solution, which would be signing off the job, would make it easy on management and easy on me. But I would be allowing the hidden cameras to be installed and permitting them to have negative effects on the lives of other employees and other people.

Quietly refusing to install the cameras would uphold the principle of confidentiality to my employer, the autonomy of management, its rights to try to catch the culprits, and the company's right to own and control its property much as the first solution would do. This solution upholds these principles because (1) it does not violate them and (2) the third solution would violate them. In begging off the case, I would leave management free to assign someone else to the task. My refusal would not violate the principle of fidelity toward my employer, because I have no obligation to carry out a job that I find ethically repugnant.

This second solution does not free me from the responsibilities I violate by the solution of following orders quietly. By begging off the job and doing nothing further, I am still an accomplice in violating the values sacrificed by the presence of the cameras. If I could have taken action to remedy the situation but did not, then I acquiesce to the violations of the principles of harm and fidelity toward my fellow workers that result from the violations of their rights and well-being by the hidden cameras.

The third solution, that of blowing the whistle and reporting the problem to the newspapers or to the union or other workers, might result in the culprits discovering the presence of the cameras. My reporting the cameras might thus hamper the company's efforts to catch the thieves.

This third solution would cause major problems for the managers, conflict for the employees, and troubles for me. I might become involved in a long and complicated debate, lose my job, or find my reputation damaged. I would receive few external rewards for pursuing such a solution and would have to have strong personal conviction to pursue it.

If I pursued this solution, I would uphold the principles of harm and fidelity toward my fellow workers, students, and others by upholding their rights to know, to act autonomously, to due process, and to freedom of expression.

This third solution would violate the principles of confidentiality and fidelity toward management by betraying its trust and exposing the confidential information. It would violate the principle of harm toward management by preventing it from protecting the equipment and catching the culprits. It would violate the company's right to protect its equipment and safeguard its ownership.

My personal conflict in the case stems from the rights to privacy, autonomy, and due process of the school employees, students, and others, on the one hand, and, on the other, the right of the administration to prevent theft and catch the thieves.

The worst thing about this case is the prospect of the company management spying on and deceiving its employees. In my opinion, a person's right to privacy is more important than catching any thieves. Violations of the right to privacy are serious affronts to the spirit of democracy, autonomy, freedom of thought, expression, and trust. They cannot be remedied by something as simple as buying a new VCR. Furthermore, there are other ways to prevent theft than installing hidden cameras that violate privacy and autonomy. Such alternate methods may be expensive and troublesome, but they are worth the cost. Management's right to catch a thief does not give it the right to use any means it chooses to obtain the desired information. To observe employees without their knowing is simply deceptive and violates the rights of the innocent. Management has taken the easy way out of a difficult problem, and in doing so it is sacrificing some fundamental ethical and political values. The end does not always justify the means.

It is worth noting here that both solutions 1 and 3 are likely to end by compromising my reputation, either by association with the installation of the cameras or by my reports of them. Only the second solution, that of begging off the case, is likely to relieve me of this association. But this solution is just as ethically objectionable as the first, and I should avoid it for the same reasons. However, it is clear that a major challenge of this situation is to figure out a way to do the right thing without seriously sacrificing my own personal reputation.

Because I disagree so strongly with management's value judgment in the case, I should act to oppose it. In doing so, however, I will try to find a way to resolve the problem while doing as little damage as possible to management's right to protect its property. Telling the newspaper would create a public issue at the expense of that right. But filing a formal complaint with the top management in the company would not necessarily harm the company.

I would write a letter to the president of the company, explain the problem, and ask that the president or board of directors address it. The company would then have the option of discussing it privately or making it public, as it chooses. If it handles the matter quietly, neither confidentiality nor my job nor reputation need suffer. Although management would surely argue that I violated the principle of fidelity toward them in this decision, I would argue that I have violated no other significant values and that I acted to prevent a far greater evil from occurring. I feel sure that upper management would want to avoid negative publicity and not allow the hidden cameras to be installed. This is an approach I could live with, knowing that I had done my best under the circumstances.

If upper management decided to go ahead with the hidden cameras and ignore my objections, I would then inform the union of their plan. As a result, the cameras could become a bargaining issue or even eventually a political one. Although I would no longer think of seeking future employment in the local community, this would not likely harm my chances of a job elsewhere. And I would have no desire to work locally anyway if I knew that the hidden cameras were in operation.

One option not addressed here is that of floating a rumor about the cameras. This might alert the employees to the risks to their privacy and cause the maintenance employees to inquire about the cameras. By such an approach, I would be acting deceptively and violating both the principles of confidentiality and fidelity to the administration. Moreover, the rumor might be traced back to me, and the thieves may even find out. Such an approach would be egoistically motivated, cowardly, deceptive, and underhanded and could do more to damage my reputation than the other options.

CHAPTER 6

Personal Ethical Problems for Analysis

1. Too Personal to Ask
Violations of Privacy in Hiring and Testing

For three years you had worked in the personnel office of Jefferson Security, a private security company that provided security guards for banks, malls, and other businesses. Your job was to interview prospective employees and administer the company's personality exam, a standard requirement in the security field. The candidates whom you interviewed had all been carefully screened for criminal records and had placed well on the aptitude tests given to every promising applicant. Your job was to judge their character through a personal interview and administer the personality exam.

Until this week you had enjoyed the job and felt confident that between the interview and the test, you were giving objective evaluations of the candidates' honesty and trustworthiness. But now there was a problem brought about by the institution of a new personality exam. Your supervisor had instructed you to use the new, "more accurate, and in-depth" exam and to do away with the old, "rather cold, and impersonal" one. You decided to review the new exam to see how much improvement had been made in the questions.

As you began reading the questions, your anticipation turned to disbelief. Some questions seemed overly personal, whereas others could not possibly be answered without reflecting poorly on anyone who replied honestly. Scanning the question booklet, you saw the following true-false questions:

Sexual things disgust me.

As a child there were times I hated my parents.

I feel like jumping off when I'm on a high place.

I have never done anything I was punished for.

I have never had black, tarry bowel movements.

There is nothing wrong with masturbating.

There is a big difference between a person who steals because he has to and a person who steals because he wants to.

I often insist on doing things my own way.

Low wages force employees to steal from their employers.

I have never taken anything home from places where I have worked in the past.

Some of the other questions required short essays and included questions very much like the true-false ones. No honest person could complete this test without looking like a thief or a liar.

As you sat and considered what to do, you remembered reading about a lawsuit brought against a company that had used just such a test. A famous Yale law professor had taken the case to court. The article included an interview in which the professor had said that such tests were seriously flawed. The answers were supposed to help employers predict future dishonest actions, but when used as criteria for hiring, they could cause a person to be denied a job without ever having done anything wrong. They were, she had said, potentially discriminatory, an unconstitutional invasion of privacy, and contained questions that were unrelated to the job or its requirements. Your new test seemed to have all those flaws and more.

You decided to talk to your supervisor. After listening to your reservations about the test, he tried to explain the theory behind the test. He said that a security job demands employees of the highest moral character and that the test is designed to evaluate a person's character. Then he enumerated three factors involved in employee dishonesty: opportunity, attitude, and need. Opportunities will always be there, and needs may arise any time in the future. But if the employee has the right attitude, he is unlikely to act dishonestly. If an employee has the attitude that dishonesty or theft is OK, then any unimportant need may trigger him to break the law. Moreover, since other security companies began using the test, the number of complaints against their guards had declined dramatically.

It sounds good in theory, you thought. But what about all those problems mentioned by the law professor? What about the invasion of an applicant's privacy? Or the fact that almost any honest person has to look bad when answering these questions truthfully? Does any employer have a right to this kind of compromising information about anyone? It would be difficult to give your own mother such information, let alone some stranger in a personnel office. And how do questions about your bowel movements, sexuality, and masturbation help predict whether you will act dishonestly?

Noting that you are bothered about administering the test, the personnel director suggested that you take the day to think it over and return tomorrow. If you felt you could not administer the test to people, he would see about giving you another assignment or transferring you elsewhere. He assured you that none of this would be held against you and that he was sure you would come to the right conclusion.

Should you administer the test or not? You wonder whether the company will hold it against you if you refuse to use the test. Besides, you genuinely enjoy doing the interviews and can't think of another job that you'd want in the company. But you are very troubled by the kinds of questions asked and the issue of privacy they raised.

By tomorrow, however, the problem must be RESOLVEDD as there will be a full waiting room of applicants at 9:00 A.M.

2. IT'S NOT MY UNION
Crossing a Picket Line

The strike at Carbon Manufacturing Company had been going on for about four weeks when you saw the ad in the paper that read, "Jobs, jobs, jobs! Carbon Manufacturing is looking for employees in all departments. High pay, benefits, no union dues. Apply at the personnel department."

Knowing that the Carbon plant was a union shop and that the strike was under way, you figured this was a temporary position with no future. Then a friend informed you that he had applied and was told that the company planned to replace the union strikers permanently. He explained that the pay was at current union levels, and benefits were pretty good. The only catch was that the company expected you never to join a union.

Because you needed a job, this all sounded very interesting. However, you were bothered by the prospect of being a scab and also by the nonunion clause. Your father had been a strong union man and had taught you about the good that unions had done for working Americans. Before unions existed, the pay was low, hours long, benefits few, and there was no job security.

Such poor working conditions, you believe, are a thing of the past, and it did not seem to you that there was still a need for unions. In fact, they seem outdated and, because of their constant unreasonable demands on management, part of the cause of our falling behind countries such as Japan, where unions did not exist or had little influence. So, lacking your father's strong commitment to unionism, you are seriously tempted to apply for a job at Carbon Manufacturing.

On the other hand, you recognize that the local union has done good things for your neighbors and that you are a part of the community that has benefited from the union's activities. Indeed, many of your family and friends are members of the union. Moreover, if you sign up as a scab, you could find yourself in the middle of some violence when crossing the picket lines. Should you apply for the job and thus undermine the union?

Your problem stems in part from the fact that you have had nothing but low-paying jobs in local burger joints and grocery stores for the last six months. Your employment problem arose after the closing of the plant where you worked as a maintenance mechanic. You are trained to fix many different kinds of machines, from lathes to punch presses and more, and genuinely resent having to sling burgers or pack bags of groceries. Lately your self-esteem has dropped in direct proportion to your time out of work. Your wife and two children have been very understanding, but you feel as though you are not doing as well for them as you were when you brought home a larger paycheck. The job you are eligible for at Carbon would pay almost as much as you were getting after three years in your previous position.

Although you have not yet made up your mind, you visit Carbon's personnel office, where your interview goes well and you are offered a job. The personnel manager explains that if the strike is settled, you will be kept on in the same position, regardless of whether the union workers return. However, the job does require that you sign a statement agreeing not to join a union as long as you are employed at Carbon.

Where do your loyalties lie? What are your priorities and obligations? Make the decision, analyzing the issues until they are RESOLVEDD.

3. IS THIS NUTRITIONAL?
Should You Work for a Tobacco Company?

Lately, you have been thinking about searching for a new job. The company you work for, Nutritional Products, Inc., was recently purchased by a large conglomerate, ABC Industries, whose major source of income (72 percent of their sales) comes from the sale of tobacco products, primarily cigarettes. Although your job and tasks have not changed since the merger, you are bothered by what you take to be a conflict of interest between your role as a nutritional researcher and the parent company's sale of cigarettes.

"How can I consider myself a health care professional and work for a company that sells a product that is known to be dangerous to the health of millions of people?" you ask Todd, your associate.

"You don't have anything to do with those sales. Why worry about it?" he replies.

"I know the dangers," you continue, "and am opposed to people smoking. We have a no smoking policy in the labs. My whole job and life's work are directed to promoting good health. Drawing a paycheck from a tobacco company seems hypocritical."

"Look, the parent company has nothing to do with the running of the daily operation here. In fact, they've left us alone and allowed us to continue just as we always have. They haven't even mentioned the negative report on tobacco products that one of the labs is doing. Clearly, they look at us just as an investment. So long as we're profitable, there's no interference."

"True, but Todd, I feel guilty about it. I can't tell you how upset I was when my grandfather died of lung cancer from smoking for fifty years. Now I'm working for a company that's selling what killed him."

"Hey, no offense, but wasn't it his choice to smoke? No one forced him. If he kept smoking after the surgeon general's report and all the negative publicity, I'd say it was his choice and he decided to take the risk. And besides, doesn't the company say that the surgeon general's report is not 100 percent proof that smoking leads to lung cancer?"

"Well, maybe, but nicotine is addictive . . ."

"Oh, wait a minute! 'Addictive' is a loaded term. If I eat five chocolate bars a day or drink ten colas, no one says I'm addicted. I can quit whenever I want. If smoking were addictive, how is it that so many people have just quit? It's a free choice. Seems to me that 'addiction' is used for someone else's habit that we disapprove of. Anyway, smoking is legal, selling cigarettes is legal, and the work you're doing here does help people, so you're not doing anything to hurt people personally. Why not just look at it that way?"

"I don't know. It bothers me," you respond.

"Enough to quit? Enough to leave in the middle of your research project? No one else here can finish that project as well as you. I think you owe some loyalty to us, too."

"I'm not sure I can look at it that way. People die from smoking—that's the bottom line."

This is a decision, calling for careful reflection and evaluation of the relevant values. What is the best thing for you to do? Analyze the case until it is RESOLVEDD.

4. HOW FAR DOES LOYALTY GO?
Can You Afford Benefits for Everyone?

Your company had grown almost overnight, it seemed, from a small machine shop to one employing over 150 people. In fact, it had been almost twenty years since you began, but only ten since you reached the present size. The nice thing about your company is that of the original fifteen people you started with ten are still with the company. It felt like family for many years, and even after the big expansion you had operated by the same rules that stressed loyalty, job security, family leaves, and a good benefits package for all your people. This reputation was one of the factors that made it easy to hire good people and keep them for so long.

Lately, however, a serious problem arose concerning the benefits package you offer your workers. With the costs of health care rising, the move to HMOs, and increased insurance costs for employers, you had run into a monetary and ethical problem. In the past eight years your treasurer, who handled all the benefits contracts, had turned to eight different insurers to get decent health care coverage for your employees. Whenever she had tried to renew a contract for coverage, the current insurer had always backed down and refused to continue coverage. The reason was always the same: you had too many "high-risk, high-cost" employees working for your company.

When the treasurer had first told of this problem, you thought it was just the one insurer who would drop coverage. However, each year for the past eight it has been the same. In looking over your workforce the insurers picked out anywhere from eight to fourteen workers who fell into the "uninsurable" category. The advice each insurer had given was to release the high-risk people and institute a hiring policy that required full disclosure of every new hiree's past medical records, as well as the usual physical exam. This way, each said, you would eliminate the high-risk employees who had either cost the insurers enormous sums of money for coverage or who were likely to do so in the near future.

The problem is that four of the employees identified by each insurer were part of the original fifteen workers who had got the company off the ground with you twenty years before. It was true, though, that each had existing medical conditions that had required very expensive care or very clearly would sooner or later. One man suffered with diabetes and kidney damage that required dialysis. His medical bills last year were close to $30,000. Another high-risk worker was a woman who had recurring cancer, requiring two mastectomies, a hysterectomy, chemotherapy, and continual monitoring. Over the years her care had run over $90,000. The other two employees were in similar situations. Indeed, these four people had used up more than anyone's fair share of the health care dollars, leading to insurers not wanting to take the risk again.

Apart from these four workers, insurers identified about ten others as falling into the high-risk category. Of this group time on the job ranges from four years to sixteen. Some haven't yet needed high-cost care but had conditions indicating they might very well become high-cost patients.

This year, your treasurer told you, it had been almost impossible to find coverage that equaled what you felt your employees were entitled to get. She had spent months calling all over the country trying to find equivalent coverage. The best she could do was another slightly downgraded package that meant employees, to stay at the same level of coverage they had, would have to pay an average of $750 a year out of their own pockets. No insurer would offer the same coverage package as the year before. This had happened four times before. The treasurer has told you that she thinks it may be impossible to find coverage next year at all. In any case the costs to the company of each new package had gone up 40 percent to 300 percent each year. Next year it could triple again! The company may not be able to afford anything like a decent package, even if an insurer willing to write the package could be found.

This was not something you wanted to happen in your "family." Your workers had always shown admirable loyalty to your company, and you had repaid it in kind with the best benefits package that could be offered. But these downgrades and the looming insurability problem has you worried. You would really hate having to cut coverage back even more because many workers cannot afford the $750 this year, let alone more next year. Besides, your coverage was always what you thought was owed to your employees. After all, they had made you a success. Without them you could not have stayed in business. You feel a duty to give them the kind of coverage you would want from an employer, and frankly, another downgrade next year wouldn't fit that description. And what if no coverage could be found?

In discussing the problem with various managers and workers, you had begun to pick up some negative feelings aimed at those few employees whose conditions had scared off previous insurers. The younger workers, especially, often commented that it seemed wrong for them to lose coverage and have to pay extra just because six or eight other employees had special medical problems. One young worker had asked directly, "How come 140 people have to suffer for the good of 10? Is that fair?" This was the crux of the issue. What is fair?

Some of the younger employees felt you should look into easing the high-risk employees out of the company. They believed it could be done humanely but firmly and quickly. Their position boiled down to the old saying "The good of the few is outweighed by the good of the many." Others said why wait—just give the employees in question two weeks' notice and a month's severance pay and that's that.

These suggestions struck you as very cruel. You understood the resentment, but not the vehemence many younger workers felt toward the older workers. The older workers knew how their coworkers felt, and a couple had even asked whether you wanted their resignations. One of those asking was Bill Plotsky, the diabetic, who had worked with you side by side from the beginning and was now head bookkeeper. This question pointed out to you how serious a problem this situation had become. Your treasurer also said other "old timers" had hinted that they'd rather quit than cause the company this kind of morale problem. A couple also felt that the company's monetary situation would be very shaky if health coverage again tripled in cost.

This was exactly why you felt you owed these older workers your loyalty. They were willing to give up their jobs rather than cause the company real monetary problems. When you spoke to them privately, though, they had all confessed that they had no real desire to leave the company, were worried that they'd never find another job given their ages and conditions, and felt that leaving would be like losing their family. Your feelings about them were pretty much the same. But do you have a choice? Is it fair to penalize every worker just because of the few who require high-cost insurance? The cost of the benefits was fast approaching the cost of the wages in the company's budget. Is it reasonable to spend more money on benefits than wages?

As you sit late one night in your office thinking about this issue, you realize that it's totally up to you to decide what to do here. You could accept the resignations, terminate the rest of the employees in question who did not offer resignations, and then find decent health care for the remaining workers. This might entail demanding access to everyone's medical records to identify all those "high-risk" workers and making such access a condition of employment in the future. All of these measures seemed to be a major violation of privacy, all just to convince some insurer that your company was worth the risk. It would also put quite a few good workers on the street. You still think you owe them better. Yet what comes first, the few? The many? The monetary status of the company? Profits? Loyalty? Privacy? Your head is beginning to spin thinking this all through. Yet you have no choice; it is up to you to see that the problem is RESOLVEDD. What is your plan?

5. So, What Are the Standards?
Hidden Promotion Requirements and Whistle-blowing

You work for Utopia Manufacturing, a medium-size company employing about 375 people, with sales around $35 million annually. Utopia produces various sorts of electrical supplies for the construction industry. It prides itself on its fairness and generosity toward its employees. Until now, you had thought this pride was well justified. However, you now have doubts about Utopia's claim of fairness and openness. You have discovered that Utopia's stated policy for determining wage increases seems to be very different from the actual practices of evaluating employees. Although the stated policy is objective and open, the actual practices make use of unstated and supposedly prohibited standards.

You are presently employed at Utopia as a skilled blue-collar worker in the machine shop, where you have worked for eight years. Following Utopia's creation of a student aid co-op program, you returned to school to finish your B.A. in business, which you had begun many years ago before dropping out. Later you completed Utopia's machinist's training program. Utopia is now paying your way toward your M.B.A. and wants to employ you in a midlevel management position once you complete your degree.

One of the classes you were required to take was business ethics. During the course, you decided to write a paper on Utopia's wage evaluation policy as an example of a fair, honest, and ethical business practice. While researching this paper, your views about fairness at Utopia had crumbled.

You had decided to analyze Utopia's guidelines for raises in Area 6, the area where you work. Three friends of yours in management agreed to help your research. You began by interviewing Danny Rose, Area 6's day shift supervisor, who was personally responsible for initiating pay raises there. During your taped interview, Danny stated, "The most important thing I look for is attitude and initiative. If an employee has those two, then I will probably grant a raise. I evaluate progress and potential, as well as productivity. But if an employee's attitude and initiative are good, though there may be problems in other areas, I wouldn't hold the employee back."

You also interviewed Celia Weinstein, plant superintendent and former Area 6 supervisor. She said, "The supervisor really knows how capable employees are. Unless I have specific knowledge to indicate that the supervisor's opinion is wrong, I approve wage increases. I don't have detailed enough information on any one employee to do a complete evaluation. But I do look for employee dependability. If I know I can count on someone's willingness to be called to work twenty-four hours a day, they'll get the raise."

Jamaal Rashid, director of human resources, works with upper management, especially the vice president of production, to determine guidelines for hiring, firing, promotions, and raises. He showed you the employee review sheet that he developed with other managers during a brainstorming session and that is used to determine all wage increases. But Jamaal pointed out that no two people are the same. Although the sheet lists only objective factors, he looks for a good attitude and desire to work as the two most important elements in determining raises. Thus, you have concluded that the three people most directly involved in the wage increase process use initiative, attitude, willingness to work, and dependability as the key factors in granting raises.

Although all this sounds fine, the problem arises from the content of the policy guidelines themselves. Listed on the evaluation sheet are (1) Time of Service, (2) Production Rate, (3) Quality of Production, (4) Knowledge of Production Methods, and (5) Continued Training. Each factor is to be rated on a scale of 1 to 10. Each of the five, moreover, is fairly easy to judge, because each involves easily quantifiable and objective factors. Nowhere on the sheet did you find the subjective factors of attitude, initiative, willingness to work, or dependability, none of which can be clearly determined on the basis of observation. However, your main worry is that these standards are all unstated. Moreover, the union contract for Area 6 employees states that such subjective considerations are *not* to be taken into account when considering wage increases.

Aided further by other friends in the office, you uncovered a confidential memo from the vice president of production to all evaluators. The memo explicitly approved the unstated standards and emphasized that they should be the most important factors in determining raises or promotions. On the other hand, the policy statement given to the union and distributed to all employees clearly states that to move from pay rate 4 up to rate 3 all that is required is four years of experience. To move from rate 3 to rate 2, one must have, in addition to six years of experience, a job proficiency rating of 8 or higher. To move from rate 2 to rate 1 requires, besides seven years of experience and a proficiency rating of 8, a rating of 8 or higher in job knowledge and evidence of continued training. None of the subjective factors were mentioned.

It became clear to you by the time you finished this research that the company uses a completely hidden set of standards, misleads the union and workers, and does so with the approval of all the managers involved in the evaluation process. There is no question that this practice is entirely unethical.

The question, however, is what you should do about it. You have taped interviews and a confidential memo as evidence. But the memo was obtained secretly, the interviews given by people you went to as friends and who trust you, while the whole project was a result of Utopia's willingness to help pay for your schooling to advance your career. On the other hand, all the blue-collar workers have been systematically lied to and are being evaluated using hidden standards to which they cannot object or reply should their raises be denied.

To whom do you owe your allegiance? How can you take steps to correct the situation without betraying the trust or jeopardizing the jobs of those who helped you? What, moreover, would be the best steps for the company to take? How could you proceed without losing your job and the education Utopia is providing you? Analyze the situation until it is RESOLVEDD.

6. DECEPTION OR SHREWD BARGAINING?
What Constitutes Unfair Contract Negotiating?

Having been a legal secretary for nearly nine years, you are familiar with many of the provisions of the American Bar Association's code of ethics and various definitions of what is considered fair bargaining in negotiations. Specifically, you know that no material facts should be withheld by either side in negotiating salaries and payments for services. Rule 4.1 of the ABA Model Rules states, "Under generally accepted conventions in negotiation, certain types of statements ordinarily are not taken as statements of material fact. Estimates of price or value placed on the subject of transaction and a party's intention as to an acceptable settlement of a claim are in this category."* You looked this up because you were bothered by the present course of your negotiations with your boss regarding your salary and bonuses for the new fiscal year. In particular, you wondered whether it was really fair for you to tell him that you would not accept anything less than an 8 percent raise and a bonus of $1,000 (10 percent more than your previous bonus), although in fact you know that you would be quite happy to get a 4 percent raise and the same bonus.

Is it a material fact that you are in reality willing to accept much less than what you told him last week? According to your grasp of the law, a material fact is one that, if known to the ignorant party, would reasonably be expected to cause that party to behave differently. It seems to you that if your boss knew you'd settle for less than you said, he would negotiate differently with you and the other partners in the law firm who must approve all raises and bonuses. Legally, fraud is involved if one party has "superior knowledge." Superior knowledge is the grasp of material facts that the other party lacks and that, without being told, the other party would be unlikely to discover.

"Surely," you think, "I am in that position when it comes to knowing that I'll settle for less. My boss can't possibly get inside my head to find this out."

---

*American Jurisprudence 2d, Fraud and Deceit, section 148.

To double-check, you asked Vera Browning, an associate in the firm and a close personal friend of yours, what she thought about all of this. She acknowledged that the ABA's code seems to exclude your intentions as material facts. However, she pointed out that, according to common law, "If one party to a contract . . . has superior knowledge that is not within the fair and reasonable reach of the other party and which the second could not discover by the exercise of reasonable diligence, or [if the first party has] means of knowledge which are not open to both parties alike, he [the first party] is under a legal obligation to speak."*

Then Vera added, "But look, we women have been too easy in negotiating here. These senior partners have been taking advantage of us because we are too polite, too timid to play the game the way they do. So my advice is that, where the law seems ambiguous, go for it, play it tough. Bluff and negotiate hard. You don't owe them a peek into your head. Would they give you one into theirs?"

All in all, you are bothered by the conflicting ethics and legality of your negotiations. On the other hand, isn't this all just part of shrewd bargaining? Surely any good salesperson keeps this kind of information under the table when he or she haggles over prices. When you bought your house, the real estate salesman quoted a price that was higher than the seller was willing to accept. You didn't see any ethical or legal problem there. In fact, when you sold some property last year, you had the same salesman handle the account because of his shrewd sales techniques.

In addition, you feel sure that your boss's initial offer is less than he is willing to pay you. So aren't you both just playing the same game? Where does shrewd, but ethical, negotiating end and fraud or unethical deception begin? According to what you know about the ABA's guidelines and legal definitions, this *could* be unethical or even fraudulent negotiating. Yet, as Vera said, the whole question of what is legal is unclear. Besides, you are sure you're worth the money you asked for, and you are sure your boss thinks so, too. Then again, he's not just a stranger: you've worked with him for seven years and gotten to know him quite well. So don't you owe it to him to be honest? Hasn't that been the key to your successful working relationship? The question that nags you now is whether he has been honest with you.

Tomorrow you have a crucial meeting with him to hammer out the final details of the raise and bonus proposal he will take to the next partners' meeting. What should you tell him? What offer should you make? You want to be fair and ethical but also want to avoid being the push-over Vera hinted you would be if you didn't stick to your first ultimatum. The problem needs to be RESOLVEDD before the meeting at 9:00 A.M. tomorrow.

7. THE PRICE OF HONESTY ▬▬▬▬▬▬▬▬
Using Your Position to Dump an Unpleasant Employee

You are the personnel manager for a manufacturing company employing 110 workers. You have held the position for two years and, except for one problem, have enjoyed the job. That problem is a worker, Davis Meany, nicknamed "the lawyer," who

---

American Jurisprudence 2d, Fraud and Deceit, section 148.

falls into the category you like to call the "if only" group, meaning "If only there were some way to get rid of this guy, I'd do it in a minute."

"The lawyer" has been with the company for almost ten years, works as a warehouse clerk, and is protected by a strong union contract. He has an annoying mastery of the details of that contract. It seems that whenever he's given an order he doesn't like, he cites some clause in the contract that gives him a way out. Often he is right, although careful scrutiny would reveal that some of his claims are misreadings of the contract. Rarely does anyone challenge him, however, because of his nasty temper and the fact that it is usually easier to assign the task to someone else.

Meany's attitude and the fact that he stands up to the bosses with impunity have lowered morale among the other warehouse employees. They think they are being forced to work harder to cover for him. On the other hand, whenever management has tried to correct the problem, the other union workers unite firmly behind "the lawyer" and assert his rights "under the terms of the contract." You suspect they are afraid that if the company forces Meany to follow orders, they will all lose some of their guaranteed protections. So they seem willing to put up with all the problems rather than compromise the contract.

Recently, Meany has been coming to work late, leaving for long washroom breaks, and sometimes going home early. The terms of the contract do not allow you to cut his pay unless he misses more than a half-hour a day, which he never does. This "five minutes here, ten minutes there" practice has also affected the attitudes of some workers, even outside the warehouse. They seem to admire his nerve in standing up to you and the bosses, and their work habits seemed to have slipped a bit, too. Other workers seem to resent his practices. But because no one will file a grievance, you are unable to do anything other than talk to him about his behavior.

Your attempts to counsel him and help improve his work habits have largely failed. Predictably, he has answered, "Show me the exact clause in the contract that says you can discipline me," or, "Where does it say that I have to see a shrink about coming in late once in a while?" You have often felt humiliated by such discussions, and you spend a lot of time after each confrontation thinking, "If only there were a way. . . ."

The plant manager, following your last discussion about the problem, shouted, "Get rid of this guy—I don't care how! I don't even want to know!"

Later that week, you received a phone call that presented a tempting opportunity. Sajid Singh, the personnel manager from a comparably sized company, located in the same town, and with which you do a small amount of business, wanted some information about a prospective employee. He told you that one of the clerks from your company has applied for a job as the warehouse supervisor at his plant. Singh asks whether you or your company would mind if he offered this clerk a job that included a raise and promotion. He is concerned that you not feel that they had "stolen one of your best workers." You are overjoyed when you learn that the clerk in question is none other than Davis Meany, "the lawyer"! You respond by saying, "We would never stand in the way of one of our employees leaving for greener pastures."

Singh says he appreciates your understanding and hopes you can help him with one final detail. He says that his company has no doubts about the man's capabilities, because he's been working in various warehouse positions for close to twenty years.

He has shown that he's a steady and trustworthy worker employed by your company for almost ten years. Moreover, he claims that your company has never had a single complaint about him. However, they need to have a strong letter of recommendation to back up their hiring him because there are two other qualified candidates still in the running, although they're the second and third choices behind Meany.

"What I need," Singh says, "is an honest evaluation of his capabilities, attitudes, and work habits to go along with his excellent résumé and successful interview." Once he receives the letter, which is really a technicality, Singh tells you, they'll be making the man "an offer he can't refuse."

Having told Singh you would get to work immediately checking out all the details and talking to everyone who would have knowledge of Meany's performance, you hang up the phone and lean back in your chair, thinking, "'If only' time is here!" Then you wonder, "Can it really be this easy? Should I really do this?" Well, should you? If they're so impressed with him and believe his representations of himself, isn't that their problem? Analyze the case until it is RESOLVEDD.

8. IT'S YOUR CHOICE
Forcing Employees to Leave a Company

You are a midlevel manager working for a giant multinational corporation that has been going through some rough economic times. Out of a total worldwide workforce of 350,000, the company has lost 34,000 employees during the past five years. The company's annual earnings estimate has fallen to below $7 a share, from last year's $10.45 a share, on earnings of $6.02 billion. New estimates for the second quarter earnings are now below $1 a share, compared with last year's $2.45, or $1.41 billion. This continues a trend begun almost five years earlier.

During the tough economic period, the company set up a voluntary program that gave incentives to employees who sought work at other companies. This was done to honor a "no firings" pledge the company had upheld ever since its founding decades before. The voluntary programs included incentives for early retirement, quitting, and expenses incurred if an employee took a job with another noncompetitive company.

Upper management now believes there is a problem with the voluntary programs. It seems that too many of the company's good workers have taken advantage of the incentives, while many weaker employees remained. An internal study done by the company's industrial psychology department concluded that productivity was down 20 percent among remaining workers, mainly because of the fact that many of the best employees had left the company.

The accounting department has recommended cutting the workforce by another 14,000 to reduce further profit loss. This has created a problem for the company: how to cut the workforce while honoring the "no firing" pledge and still hang on to the best workers.

On your desk is a memo from the highest level stating that a new policy is in effect. The memo outlines a program that allows managers to "encourage" certain targeted employees to leave the company. The memo also notes that many of the weaker employees have been laid off indefinitely, thereby technically adhering to the no-firing policy. However, a certain number of targeted employees cannot be laid off because of the terms of their contracts. It is these employees who you are being told to "encourage" to leave. Attached to the memo is a list of four expendable employees who work in your department. The list ends with the statement "You are to convince said employees that seeking employment elsewhere would be to their best interest."

Through the managers' grapevine, you learn that a dim view will be taken of midlevel managers who cannot "encourage" the targeted employees to move on. As you contemplate the memo and the pressure being put on you and the other managers, it strikes you that at least two of the employees named on your list are people whose work you have always considered to be well above average. Not on the list are two people whose work you believe is marginal. No guidelines or reasons are given explaining how the company decided who would be placed on the list and who would not.

The whole situation has you deeply troubled. You think that this is a violation of the spirit of the no-firing policy. Yet you are aware of the fact that the best hope for the company's continued economic survival is to cut back its workforce. You are also bothered by the two people on the list who do not deserve to be eliminated and who have considerable value to the company. Finally, you have no real idea of how to go about "encouraging" people to leave jobs they have held, in all four cases, for at least five years.

After speaking to the head of personnel about the policy and your questions, you are still unsure of how to proceed. She told you that it was really up to you how to convince the employees to leave. Furthermore, if you feel that some of the people on your list are there by mistake, you must prepare a memo outlining your objections and suggesting alternate names that might replace them on the list. She also notes that employees who leave will be given two weeks' severance pay for every year they've worked at the company. But this offer is good only for those who leave voluntarily before the end of the next month. After that, there will be no severance pay for employees who leave voluntarily or who are fired. Your job is to inform marginal employees who want to stay that their pay may be cut or that they may be fired eventually.

It seems clear to you that the company is not simply encouraging voluntary participation. Rather, it is pressuring certain employees into quitting. The token adherence to the no-firing policy seems to be a mere sham. On the other hand, should you fail to carry out company orders, you may well be looked upon as marginal.

Several options are possible. You may adhere to the list, refuse to do the company's dirty work, or come up with some better way of handling your situation. Which is best, and for what reasons? Analyze the case until it is RESOLVEDD.

9. A Spy in the House
The Leaking of Trade Secrets

Returning from a meeting of Galesburg Data Corporation's area supervisors, you can't stop wondering about the people you thought you knew and could trust. You worry about the six people in your own research group. "Someone is leaking new product information to our competitor. It's got to be one of them because it sure isn't me," you think as you pull up your chair and sit down to look over the personnel files of the six people who work for you.

After reviewing the files for about thirty minutes, you are narrowing in on Marcia Poston. There it is, staring you in the face: Marcia's husband, Tony, works for PLUSDATA, not exactly a rival company, but one that previously developed some products related to your group's research. Tony Poston is listed as a "data systems specialist" at PLUSDATA. At the meeting PLUSDATA was discussed in detail, because they are publicizing a new data retrieval system that is almost a clone of the one your research group is working on.

On the other hand, Marcia has been working with you for eleven years, eight before she married Tony. She always seemed to be the most trustworthy person in the group, and you can hardly imagine her telling Tony any of your company's trade secrets.

Perhaps it is someone else in the group, a disgruntled employee such as Zeke Lesser, who had been turned down for promotion and had been job searching before deciding to stick it out at Galesburg. Had he interviewed at PLUSDATA? You don't know. You wonder, "Should I ask Zeke where he interviewed? Do I have the right to know? What if he tells me to bug off? But what if he says he did interview there? Can I conclude from just this that he's selling us out?" You just aren't sure what to do. It doesn't seem likely that Zeke would be that sneaky or that upset about his job. But it also doesn't seem possible that Marcia could be giving away the information PLUS-DATA must have used to develop their system. Nobody else in the group is really a possibility because they just don't have access to the right kind of information.

You wonder how you can handle this so you don't insult anyone, create a climate of distrust, or give away your suspicions. You decide to call everyone, one by one, into your office over the next few days, explain the situation, and see what you can pick up on the matter. Perhaps you will detect some telltale signs of uneasiness in Marcia or Zeke.

During your interview with Zeke, you decide that he's in the clear. He points out that he had never interviewed with PLUSDATA because he'd had a bad experience with them during an interview years before. "A bunch of SOBs! Only an idiot would work there" were his exact words. You wonder whether he knows about Marcia's husband working there, but you just chuckle to yourself and let it pass. But this does seem to leave Marcia as the only likely source of the leak.

The next day you meet with Marcia. After explaining the problem, you ask, "Is there any possibility that you know who could be leaking the information?" She answers that she has no idea at all.

"Doesn't your husband work for PLUSDATA? What exactly does he do there?" you ask.

"Yes, he works there as a data systems analyst, but you don't think I'd tell him anything about the details of our work here, do you? Sure, I complain about this or that and tell him whether the work is going well or not, but no technical details."

"Could he be putting two and two together and figuring out what we're doing here?"

"Look, Tony's not like that; he'd never do things that way. Look somewhere else. I don't like the insinuation that I'm leaking information or he's spying on us.

What do you figure, he's some sort of secret agent who married me to pry out our trade secrets?"

After apologizing for being too blunt, you explain that this is the only explanation that makes sense and that you never thought Marcia was leaking secrets or doing anything deliberately wrong. But if Marcia and Tony talk about work at home, couldn't Tony remember a good idea, forget where it came from, and think it was his own idea? "Maybe you'd better just not talk about work at all," you suggest.

Marcia says angrily, "That's crossing the line. You can't tell me what to talk to my husband about at home! We relax by talking about our days. If we couldn't do that, we'd go nuts with all this secrecy to worry about. We think of each other as one person, parts of the same whole, and I'm not going to stop talking about my problems with Tony. I don't tell him anything technical about our work. And he does not try to figure out what I'm doing. Zip, zero, end of discussion. If you bring it up again, I'll quit and really take my trade secrets with me. There's no law against that, is there?"

Now what are your options? What should you do to RESOLVE the situation at hand?

10. SPYING THE SPIES ▬▬▬▬▬▬▬▬▬▬▬▬▬
Should You Report a Coworker's Personal Discussions?

You worked at Galesburg Data for almost six years without anything like this happening. It struck you as very odd. Your supervisor talked to four other workers from your area in the last two days, all very "hush, hush." The supervisor had never called you in for a "heart-to-heart talk" before, but today that changed.

As you left your supervisor's office, you wondered why she had asked you whether you discuss work-related problems with anyone. What was going on? Why did she ask you about your knowledge of what the other people in your area were working on? The supervisor had never raised such questions before. And then she rambled on about company loyalty for almost ten minutes. It just seemed weird.

Sitting at your desk near the supervisor's office, you kept thinking about events during the past month or so. It was pretty obvious something was going wrong. Then all those interviews and questions. Company loyalty? Was someone quitting, taking their knowledge of trade secrets with them?

That's it! That's what it's all about—the new project, PLUSDATA's newly announced retrieval system. It all fit. Someone had leaked information.

Just as you reached that conclusion, you saw Marcia Poston going into the supervisor's office. Something clicked. You recalled a lunch you had with Marcia and her husband about three months ago. At the time, Marcia had gone on and on about the developments in her work on Galesburg's new retrieval system. She kept asking you about your role in the project, too. You recalled nothing out of the ordinary, just the usual "shop talk." But her husband, Tony, was there, and you now realize that she had told you he worked for PLUSDATA!

Other conversations ran through your mind, and you remember at least three other times that Marcia talked about confidential information in front of her husband. None of it was anything more than harmless talk between coworkers, and she probably wasn't even aware of doing it. But there was no denying that Tony was there and probably heard more than he should have. Did Marcia talk to Tony about work-related things when they were alone? How much detail may she have given him? You can't imagine her "selling out" Galesburg. And Tony does not seem like the kind of guy who would be trying to steal trade secrets from his own wife. But it still seems to fit.

Should you tell the supervisor about your suspicions? Is there enough evidence? All you have are impressions and unreliable memories about casual conversations. Suppose you're wrong about what's going on? Suppose you're right about the problem but wrong about Marcia? Won't this hurt her both professionally and personally? How much do you owe Galesburg or your supervisor? How much do you owe Marcia, your colleague and friend? Perhaps it's best to let the supervisor do the digging and to stay out of it altogether. You are just not sure. To make a decision, you should analyze the issue until RESOLVEDD.

11. A MARTINI FOR ROSSI ▬▬▬▬▬▬▬▬▬
Alcohol on the Job and Whistle-blowing

Edgar Rossi could have no way of knowing that you were looking for him or that the reassembly of an important piece of machinery for the production line was being delayed by his absence. The boss did not know that Rossi had not returned from lunch, as he was in a production meeting that had started during your lunch hour. But you had noticed Rossi's absence about fifteen minutes after your lunch was over.

You had just finished working on the roller bearings of the plastic molding machine. Rossi was supposed to help you on the next step when you realized that he wasn't back. This was the last step in the repair, and the other shop workers had moved temporarily to other jobs in the plant. As a result, no one was available to ask about Rossi's locale. In addition, no one was present to fill in for Rossi, and you weren't able to do the complicated rewiring that was his specialty.

At this point, your only choice was to search the plant for him. After looking for about twenty minutes, you bumped into Jane Howard, a good friend of Rossi's. "Have you seen Ed lately, Jane?"

"Not since lunch. I left early, but Ed stayed over at Gillard's with a friend he met there, a guy he hadn't seen for five years, who just walked in as we were leaving."

You decided that you had to check out Gillard's, a local bar and grill that is a popular lunch spot with the plant workers. You trotted down the block, entered Gillard's, and found Rossi sitting at the bar with another man.

"Rossi, come on, we've got work to do—now," you said, after exchanging greetings with both men.

"Oh, geez, is it that late?" Rossi answered, with his words slightly slurred and the smell of liquor on his breath.

"Yeah, but Mr. Locus isn't back from his meeting yet, so he hasn't noticed you were gone."

You both ran back to the shop and completed the work before Mr. Locus, the boss, returned from his meeting. However, Rossi was in no shape to do the work as well or as quickly as he should have. So you took over a lot of it and just followed his instructions. As a result, it took much longer than usual. Although the machine was back on line by four o'clock, you knew it would have been there at least an hour earlier if Rossi had not taken his long lunch. As everyone at the plant knows, every hour the line is down costs the company about $80,000. You felt guilty about the delay, though you realized it was not your fault.

Normally, this sort of thing would not have bothered you. But Rossi had been missing last week, and you covered for him then, too. Moreover, other workers had been complaining about Rossi's erratic behavior for the last six months. You had smelled liquor on his breath more than once, a couple of times at the beginning of the day. Although none of the managers have noticed Rossi's absences, your coworkers figure it is just a matter of time.

As you talked this over with your wife, a psychologist, she frowned and then said that it sounded like Ed Rossi was either an alcoholic or well on his way to becoming one. When she listed the symptoms of alcoholism, you pointed out that Rossi's recent behavior fit the mold pretty well. She then said that the most recent statistics she had seen, which were somewhat outdated, indicated that alcoholics cost American businesses close to $55 billion a year in lost production, health coverage, accidents, crime, and welfare costs. Part of the problem, she explained, was that other workers try to cover up for their friends, and the problems continue longer than they should.

The next day at work you confronted Rossi tactfully about his behavior and his drinking. You stated that you didn't know for sure that he had a drinking problem but that everyone suspected it. He vehemently denied having a problem with alcohol, saying you were just "uptight" because of yesterday's close call. He reassured you that it would not happen again.

Things went well for about three weeks. Rossi was always on time, you did not smell any liquor on his breath, and he took no more long lunches. But then, when you were assigned, along with Nick Battle and Rossi, to fix a hydraulic lift, Rossi was absent again. There was no way the two of you could do the job, as it involved holding a large hydraulic piston in place while someone tightened the clamps that held the assembly. Weighing three hundred pounds and awkwardly positioned, the piston required two strong workers to hold it.

"Where's Rossi?" Nick practically bellowed.

"I'll see if I can find him," you responded. This time you went immediately to Jane to ask whether Ed had been at lunch with her. She said he hadn't but had heard him say he was going over to Gillard's with Paul. Paul said he had lunch with Ed over an hour ago but that Ed had stayed at Gillard's, saying he was entitled to a three-martini lunch just like the executives. A quick call to Gillard's confirmed Rossi's presence. But this time, speaking on the phone, he refused to return to work, claiming he was sick. By the slurring of his words and his belligerent tone, you figured he was drunk.

"Well, I say it's time to blow the whistle on Mr. Rossi. I'm sick of people covering up for him," Nick said seriously when you told him the situation. "What do you say, are you with me? After all, you've got the facts. Let's get Mr. Locus and get it over with."

Should you go along with Nick? So far, none of the bosses know about Rossi, and they may ignore your complaint. Perhaps you owe Rossi one more chance, since you can't be sure he's an alcoholic. On the other hand, his behavior is starting to affect morale and put you in a bad position. He is definitely costing the company money in lost production time. Consider the options available, the values at stake, and address the problem until it is RESOLVEDD.

12. TO REWARD OR RETIRE
Does Past Contribution Count for Nothing?

You work at a small manufacturing facility as a middle manager responsible for three teams of employees, each with its shop floor manager in charge of minute-by-minute operations. In an effort to eliminate all questions of age discrimination, your parent company, which owns the facility, has eliminated all mandatory retirement policies. It has instituted a rigorous system of regular evaluations of all employees to be carried out quarterly. The local union has approved the evaluations, which are causing considerable extra work for management at all levels.

For the past year, you have heard disturbing rumors about your oldest shop supervisor, Milton Bailey. Last spring, some workers complained that he had lost a number of their completed job assignment worksheets and had then blamed them for not turning in the completed forms after finishing their jobs. This fall, three of his workers have expressed to you in an informal way the concern that he seems a little out of touch, rambling on while giving out work assignments, and often losing track of which workers are performing which jobs. Such criticisms have reached your immediate superior, Marlene Burley, the plant superintendent, who has asked you to investigate.

At sixty-eight years old, Milt has spent his entire career at this facility. When he began nearly forty-five years ago, it was a small, independent operation that employed less than one-fifth of the workers it does now. In those days, it produced only one-tenth of its present volume and demanded little technical skill of its managers. Milt worked his way to the supervisory level on the strength of his ability to work well individually with small groups of employees. Since he became a supervisor, Milt's team has doubled in size, and his job has grown to require more technical expertise. Milt's first love is his personal involvement with each job. As he says, "I'm a hands-on guy, not some desk jockey." But the increased team size and technical nature of his work have reduced the impact of his personal touch. In the past, he had always received above-average performance reviews and enjoyed the loyalty of his workers. Lately, however, his performance reviews rate his work largely as "adequate," and complaints from his subordinates, especially the more recently hired skilled workers, have increased.

Milt has been a model employee throughout his career, always willing to work overtime and use his considerable human relations skills to mediate between management and employees during labor disputes. Moreover, when your company was purchased by a conglomerate three years ago, Milt was a moving force in making the transition from independent company to corporate subdivision. It was he who calmed the fears of many workers who worried that the takeover meant the loss of their jobs.

He strongly supported retaining you in your position after the merger. In fact, he wrote glowing reviews of your work for the new management. In your opinion, the company, the employees, and you personally owe this man a debt of gratitude. Perhaps it was a sense of this sentiment that led management to grant Milt an exception to the mandatory retirement policy still in effect two years ago.

But that was then and now is now, Marlene Burley points out. Gratitude and efficiency are two different things. She has ordered you to do a thorough evaluation of Milt and give her a recommendation next week on just what to do in his particular case.

When you paid a surprise visit to his area last week, you found his performance competent enough, although he did seem to be a little annoyed and unresponsive to a worker's suggestions about who to assign to a particular job. He also seemed a little distracted and absent-minded, which reminded you of the time last month when he gave rather vague reasons for missing an entire scheduled meeting with you.

You later mentioned the topic of retirement in the course of a casual conversation with Milt, and he was visibly distressed. At first he insisted, rather defensively, that he would himself know when he no longer had the ability or energy to do his job. He also indicated in subdued tones that his job had been the most essential part of his daily life since his wife had died two years ago. For him, he said, retirement was not something he ever thought about or wanted.

Your report is nearing completion, and your findings are clear: Milt's performance is falling although he has made no serious mistakes as yet. As his absent-mindedness, unresponsiveness and moments of annoyance increase, he will clearly be losing the confidence of his subordinates. And as they complain more and he ultimately makes a costly mistake or two, the cost of removing him too late will increase.

Marlene has already made her ideas clear to you, saying that it is better to trim dead wood sooner than later. Of course, she has only worked here for two years, arriving well after the takeover. She lacks your understanding of what Milt has given to this facility and your sense of loyalty to Milt, as do his young, technically trained subordinates. Indeed, like many companies in the era of takeovers, restructuring, and downsizing, this one has clearly deemphasized the importance of loyalty to both employees and the company.

So now you have a problem in deciding what to recommend to Marlene. She has already given you excellent evaluations and has hinted that she will be recommending you for a raise if your good work continues. But what is the best way to handle a case like that of Milton Bailey? Should there be a place in employee policy for appreciation of past contribution and loyalty? And how could one make such a case to today's managers who are under world-competitive pressure to promote the bottom line? These are value questions with important ethical components that need careful analysis and evaluation if the case is to be best RESOLVEDD.

13. Build to Suit ▬▬▬▬▬▬▬▬▬▬▬▬▬▬▬▬▬▬
Can You Afford to Hire a Disabled Worker?

Marcia Yellow Eagle was clearly the best-qualified applicant you had interviewed in the last two weeks. You were looking for a good architect to add to your construction company, but you also knew the costs of hiring Marcia.

Marcia was the first candidate you interviewed. She impressed you with her résumé and letters of recommendation. She had an M.A. from one of the top three schools of architecture in the nation, six years of experience with two well-known architects, and training in structural engineering beyond what most architects possessed. None of the other candidates came close to these qualifications.

However, there was a drawback. Marcia was unable to walk and sat in a wheelchair. She explained that she could use her crutches to get around a bit but that she seldom bothered as she was very comfortable getting around in her wheelchair. But you did not see her disability as a problem. The problem was, ironically, architectural.

When Marcia said that she had a very hard time getting to your office for her interview, she expressed some surprise that a construction company would occupy a building that did not have any access for wheelchairs. You explained that the building was over sixty years old and that you had never employed anyone who used a wheelchair. She understood but also said that if she were to accept this job, an elevator and other structural changes would have to be installed. Without such changes she would simply not accept a job with your firm.

Being an architect, she was able to explain exactly what was needed. And as a construction company owner, you knew exactly what such modifications would cost. To install the elevator, alter the existing building to accommodate it, plus make the other necessary adaptations, would run over $200,000. When you asked Marcia whether she would consider starting before the modifications were made, she had said yes. But unless they were done within a few months, she added, she would have to quit.

At that point in the interview process you told her you would weigh her requests when considering who to hire but that she was still one of your top candidates. Now, however, it was clear that she was the only candidate any reasonable employer would consider. The other three candidates were good, but nowhere near Marcia in ability or experience.

Without the need to modify your building, which you owned, there would be no doubt about who to hire. At this point, however, it just doesn't look like you can afford the modifications. On the other hand, can you afford to let Marcia slip through your fingers? Then there was always the possibility of a lawsuit for discriminating against the disabled, though perhaps no one would ever know why you decided not to hire Marcia.

You knew that Marcia could add so much to your company that it seemed foolish not to hire her. But your treasurer explained that an expenditure of $200,000 right now would place the company on very thin ice for at least a year. A major financial setback or lost contract could put you in the red. Deep down you knew that if you didn't hire Marcia, the reason would be solely because she was disabled or, rather, that because she was disabled you could not afford to hire her. But aren't these really the same? There was simply no way to look at this as a black-and-white decision. It is a decision that requires thought to be RESOLVEDD.

14. IT'S HIS COMPANY, BUT... ■■■■■■■■■■
Gender Discrimination and a Promotion

John Damien is the president of a medium-sized printing company that he started from scratch over twenty years ago. Rachel Lesser has worked for John's company for the last four years and has reached a turning point in her career. At the present executive meeting, she is being considered for promotion to vice president. If promoted, she would be the first woman to reach that level in the company. However, a struggle is brewing.

Rachel began four years ago as a salesperson, dealing mostly with small clients and companies that were placing a single order. She prided herself on treating everyone as if they were longtime customers. As a result, many of the new clients did become steady customers. Rachel's sales expertise increased John's business substantially in the next two years.

During the last two years, Rachel continued to sell printing but also took over a good deal of the office management at the print shop. John had always been a bit disorganized when it came to the details of everyday operations. Rachel began helping with one or two loose ends, and she went on to cover more and more of the everyday business of the company. John was increasingly able to work with the printers and graphics art department, his two specialties.

Eventually, on your recommendation, John made Rachel sales manager, with a raise and bonus. Although she rarely worked directly with John, who was hardly ever in the office, John trusted your judgment enough to promote her. The company is now running much more efficiently.

You are now vice president in charge of accounts, personnel, and purchasing, having risen to that position over the past ten years. You have a good working relationship with John and feel as though you understand and trust him well. This is one reason for your success in the firm. Now, however, you are faced with an extremely touchy situation.

At the last executive meeting, you proposed that Rachel be promoted to the rank of vice president. You gave a positive presentation that the other three executives found convincing. John, however, spoke up, abruptly opposing it. Because of his position as president, John's opposition was a veto. To your satisfaction, the other executives joined you in objecting to John's veto. As a result, John said that he would consider it for a week and announce his decision at the next meeting. That meeting took place earlier today, and you are still reeling from it all.

John began the current meeting by explaining that he just could not promote Rachel. He was not, he insisted, biased against women. He explained, however, that he had never been able to work closely with women without becoming nervous and inhibited in his job. That was the reason there had never been another female executive. He apologized for seeming to be sexist, explaining that it was not a prejudice but a simple fact: a phobia, according to his therapist. Indeed, he explained, his feelings ran so deep that even therapy had failed to improve his ability to work with women. Because he would have to work closely with any vice president on major issues, he could not take the chance of promoting Rachel. If he could not work effectively, the business would suffer.

You had argued, at the meeting, that in her new capacity, Rachel would not be doing much more than in the past. John had responded that she would be at weekly meetings, be consulted on all major contracts and negotiations, and meet with him regularly for all kinds of things that vice presidents do. At that point, you had suggested just giving her the promotion and raise, without any new responsibilities and without her having to attend the weekly meetings. John pointed out that it would be bad business to pay for a vice president who did no more than a sales manager. In addition, it would be bad for her morale to promote her to executive level without executive responsibilities or privileges. It was better, he said, not to promote her, especially since she didn't know that she was being considered. "No harm, no foul" was the way he put it. "Just keep the whole thing confidential and no one gets upset."

Nothing you said would change John's mind. Although you think this is unfair to Rachel, you can hardly blame John. After all, you think, it isn't exactly his fault. It's a psychological problem he is trying to overcome, and he deserves credit for that much. At first, you accepted John's explanation that he is not prejudiced—he is going on past experience. And the business surely would suffer if John couldn't do his job efficiently. But you were still troubled by your conviction that Rachel deserved the promotion and could do more for the company if she received it.

As you were walking out of the meeting, Rachel stopped you and asked to speak with you in private. "I heard a rumor that something big concerning me was coming up at the meeting today," she said.

"I can't discuss the meeting at all, Rachel," you said. "These meetings are private. Execs only, you know." The excuse sounded weak as you said it.

Rachel picked up on your uneasiness and kept asking about what went on and how it affected her. She said that if she was being discussed, for better or worse, she had a right to know. What should you say to her—today, tomorrow, or later?

She does not accept the claim of confidentiality. She pointed out that you yourself hinted strongly that something important would happen to her. Should you tell her what happened? How could you explain it if you did? Could she have grounds for a lawsuit? Suppose she asked you to testify against John? There are so many awkward and troublesome angles that you could be caught up in. And how would John react to what may appear as a "betrayal"? What do you owe John, the company, and Rachel? Much will have to be sorted through before you can make a responsible decision and have the situation RESOLVEDD.

15. LOSE IT OR LEAVE IT ▮▮▮▮▮▮▮▮▮▮▮▮▮▮▮
Is Being Overweight a Good Reason for Discharge?

Becky Darrien worked as an emergency room nurse at Bigtown Hospital until she was suspended pending the decision by a three-member board of review. The hospital has arranged for a hearing to help the board determine whether she should be terminated. You have been asked to serve on the board of review as the representative of Becky's peer group.

You have been an administrator at Bigtown for almost eight years and have a nodding acquaintance with Becky. You do not, however, work with her or know her except to say "Hi" in the halls. The other members of the board are Dr. Lord, a staff surgeon, and Mrs. Hines, a senior nurse supervisor who does not know Becky.

The problem before the board involves Becky's weight. She is 5'5" tall and weighs 330 pounds. When she began at Bigtown Hospital four years ago, she had weighed 240 pounds. During her preemployment interviews, she had stated that she had lost thirty pounds during her senior year as a nursing student because her school had a limit on how much a nursing student could weigh. The school had taken the position that some nursing functions require that nurses be physically fit. Moving patients and administering cardiopulmonary resuscitation (CPR), for example, require strength and agility. Becky had failed to pass her physical during her senior year and had agreed to go on a school-supervised weight loss program, during which she lost the thirty pounds the school regulations required.

Following her graduation, she joined the nursing staff at Bigtown and began to put on the weight she had lost. Now, four years later, she weighs 330 pounds, despite being put on a hospital-administered weight control program over nine months before.

The hospital, like the school of nursing, has strict physical fitness requirements for its staff. Becky is nowhere near the weight guidelines for someone her height. The hospital rules require her to weigh 230 pounds or less, and she had been hired with the understanding that she would lose weight. During her weight loss program, however, she gained forty-five pounds. The hospital administration has decided that Becky cannot perform her job effectively because of the limits on her physical endurance and mobility caused by her weight. The administration has stated that Becky was granted sufficient time to lose the necessary weight, has failed, and it is now appropriate that she be terminated. The termination order has been submitted to the three review board members as required by the nurses' contract.

During the early testimony to the board, the hospital lawyer argued that Becky had violated her contractual obligations to maintain her fitness for duty and that therefore the hospital no longer had any obligation to honor her contract, which runs for another eight months. Furthermore, the lawyer pointed out that her weight prevents her from performing her duties adequately in the emergency room, where she works. She had, on a couple of occasions, become faint and breathless during particularly long emergency CPR sessions, which lasted almost an hour each. In each case, another nurse had taken over her job while she rested.

The hospital lawyer further argued that the hospital has an obligation to its patients to maintain high standards of performance for its staff. Additionally, some nurses who testified thought that it may well be best for Becky to avoid work that makes such heavy physical demands. Thus, perhaps everyone would benefit in the long run from her being released.

Becky argues, on the other hand, that she is fit for her job and is being discriminated against because of a social stigma attached to overweight people. She claims that forty-five minutes of CPR would exhaust any of the members of the board and that many trim, fit nurses cannot go that long without a break. Becky maintains that she has substantially performed her contractual obligations. As far as the violation of her obligation to lose weight, Becky believes that she is an addictive personality and cannot stop eating because of a genetic condition that is beyond her control. You are aware of recent studies that indicate that some people suffer from the sort of condition Becky describes. Moreover, some researchers have described such a condition and classified it as a disease like alcoholism. She believes that because she has no control over her weight, the hospital is punishing her for something she is not responsible for, thus violating her right to just and fair treatment. But you are not at all sure that Becky falls into this category because she has not presented any evidence to back up her claim.

After the hearings and discussion, Dr. Lord votes to keep Becky on staff until the end of her eight-month contract; if she loses the weight, he will vote to give her a new contract; if not, he recommends another hearing. Mrs. Hines votes for termination, rejecting the idea that Becky has no control over her weight. Even if the claim were true, Mrs. Hines says, the fact remains that Becky had not passed the physical required for continued employment. She adds, "Our obligations are to the patients first, and if she isn't fit enough to do her job, the patients suffer." You ask for some time to think before voting.

Yours will be the deciding vote, and you have the evening to think it over. Taking all pertinent values and possible consequences into account, what would be best? Analyze the case until it is RESOLVEDD.

16. SHOULD I LEAVE OR MAKE UP? ▬▬▬▬▬▬
Personal Appearance and Company Policy

You had been working as a travel agent for more than a year. You couldn't believe it when you first got the pink slip in your paycheck envelope. You had been fired! What amazed you even more was that the cause was your refusal to wear makeup on the job. Now you are trying to decide whether to sue your former employer.

You have been talking recently to representatives of the Americans for a Free Workplace (AFFW), a group similar to the American Civil Liberties Union. The AFFW had contacted you to encourage you to pursue a lawsuit for wrongful discharge.

To think this had happened when all you had wanted was a nice job at a travel agency, to earn a little money, meet people, and work part-time so you'd have time to spend at home with your three-year-old daughter. At first the whole thing seemed silly, but as you thought about it, you realized that a number of important rights and principles were at stake.

You took the part-time (twenty-five hours a week) job as a travel agent with Cheapo Travel Agency over a year before, partly because it seemed to be a moderately sized corporation (250 employees at ten national locations) with a sense of humor. "Just look at their name," you had thought when noting the employment ad in the paper. During your interview it seemed like just the place you were looking for. The managers you had talked to did have a sense of humor and had no disagreement at all with your working part-time or with juggling your schedule to fit the needs of your daughter, Christine. They especially liked your previous experience as a real estate salesperson and your manner of dealing with people. They hired you right on the spot.

An employee group, though not a union, asked you to join despite the fact that you were only part-time and not really eligible for membership. This group did not negotiate contracts or require dues but did consult with management in the making of policies for the agency and its workers. It was the action of the employee group, however, that led to your firing.

This group had agreed with management that the company's image needed to be improved, to have a more glamorous and "European" feel. Most of the improvements were matters of changing the names of vacation packages to sound more European, the decor of the offices, and other rather superficial measures. However, at the suggestion of the employee group's female officers, the company had adopted an appearance standard that included the rule that women employees who deal directly with the public must wear "at least a minimum amount of makeup." Male employees were required to wear suits and ties that reflected current European fashion standards.

You had refused to wear makeup, saying that you had never worn it in your life and were not about to start at thirty-six years of age. Upon stating your refusal, you had been asked to meet with a committee composed of management and representatives of the employee group. During the meeting, you explained that you had nothing against makeup or people who wore it but didn't use it yourself and didn't wish to start using it. One of the managers, Mike Redstone, explained that the policy was meant simply to present a "continental European look" to the customers, thus giving them a flavor of the style and elegance of France, where most women were known to wear makeup. He added that this was the reason the male employees would wear "French-style" suits and ties. Marge Doctrowe, the employee group's president, told you that the idea for the makeup rule came from the group's executive council, which had suggested the idea to management.

"It was our choice, you see, and you are a member of the group, so you shouldn't look at this as something the company forced on you," Marge concluded.

"Do you think I don't look good enough to sell European vacation plans? Don't I have a right to dress and look the way I want to look, so long as it isn't outrageous or harmful to business?" you asked.

Everyone in the group had responded that you are a highly professional worker and an attractive representative of the company. They all agreed, however, that the rule must apply to everyone. When you again declined to adopt the policy, Mike offered you a job confirming reservations and flights, a phone job behind the scenes, but at your normal salary and work schedule. Following your second refusal, the meeting was terminated.

A week later, the pink slip appeared in your pay envelope. You then filed a formal grievance. But the grievance review committee, composed primarily of the same people you had met with earlier, denied the appeal. One member, Bart Lincoln, had been adamant in his defense of your personal autonomy. He argued that requiring makeup seemed to be left over from the old days when "women were expected to be glamorous even on the job."

You suspected that Bart had contacted the AFFW's lawyers, who then contacted you to encourage you to file suit for wrongful discharge. The AFFW lawyer, Michelle Permenter, argued that you should file suit because this is an issue of women's choice and privacy, a matter not just of personal autonomy but of the rights and freedoms of all women workers. You are not sure you want to go this far but recognize the larger issues beyond your own case.

Should you file the suit? Is this really a serious rights issue, or are you just being stubborn? Are you bound by the rules freely adopted by the employee group and presented by it to management? What are the central issues? How should you react? Analyze the case until it is RESOLVEDD.

17. AFFIRMATIVE ACTION ▪▪▪▪▪▪▪▪▪▪▪▪▪▪▪▪▪▪▪▪▪▪
Qualifications, Seniority, and Affirmative Action

You are on a five-member panel assigned to review three workers' files for a promotion decision. The company you work for has a policy of worker participation in hiring, promotion, and firing decisions that was implemented as part of its union contract. The panel also includes another fellow union employee, a salaried worker, a member of management, and the director of personnel. And, just your luck, the situation is a sticky one.

Three union members are applying for promotion to the position of production line supervisor. Dale Riggs, Martha Gale, and Marcus Washington were all hired at about the same time, with Dale having two weeks' seniority over Martha, and Martha about eight days' seniority over Marcus. All three have been employed as line workers on the same assembly line, and each is considered a valuable worker.

Marcus is a black man, hired under the company's affirmative action program. This program was voluntarily instituted by the company. The union advocated the program and made concessions to get it adopted by the company. The union agreed to downplay seniority in the promotion process to further the goals of affirmative action.

Because Dale and Martha have seniority and Marcus is a member of a racial minority, promoting either Dale or Martha may be taken as upholding seniority and thus as a compromise of the affirmative action policy. On the other hand, although seniority may be overruled for the sake of affirmative action, seniority is still a time-honored and important principle for the union. It must not be taken too lightly or ignored completely. The union wants seniority to remain as important as any other requirement for promotion. In the eyes of the union, a compromise of seniority might set a dangerous precedent, because management would like to drop seniority altogether as a criterion for promotion.

Can you apply either affirmative action guidelines or seniority in the case without being unfair to someone? You don't think so. You wonder, therefore, whether Martha is a good compromise candidate.

During the discussion of the candidates, it is generally agreed that, judging by their performance, all are well qualified for the promotion. However, the other members believe that Dale is slightly better qualified than Martha, who is slightly better qualified than Marcus. However, no one on the panel believes the differences in their job performance are significant. Although everyone likes and respects Dale and Martha, Marcus seems to interact best with the other workers and managers. His congeniality could be a real asset in performing his job. You are fairly sure, though, that Dale and Martha are almost equally easy to work with.

The preliminary vote shows that one panel member firmly believes that Dale is entitled to the promotion because he has done the best work of the three and has slightly more seniority. Another member clearly favors Marcus on grounds of affirmative action. A third member wants to promote Martha because her qualifications seem slightly better than Marcus's, though less than Dale's, and, she says, because women are underrepresented in supervisory roles in the plant. In addition, she says, Title VII of the Civil Rights Act indicates that, like racial minorities, women are a protected class covered by affirmative action guidelines.

Your fellow union employee and you are concerned about the whole situation and believe in the seniority principle, giving Dale the edge. But you also believe that a matter of a few days seems largely insignificant when considering such an important promotion. Furthermore, you both recognize that to abandon the affirmative action policy, adopted after a long fight on the union's part, would send the wrong message to black employees, who are also underrepresented in supervisory roles. You realize that affirmative action covers both Marcus and Martha but also that the company has never discriminated against women, while it has a poor record of hiring and promoting black workers. Yet, Marcus was hired with affirmative action in place, and you wonder whether that's all he's entitled to or whether affirmative action applies to every decision involving him from now on. The other union panelist says she will abide by your decision since you've been at the company as a union employee for almost twenty-five years.

How can you best decide the case? Which principles play the most important role in the case: seniority, performance, or affirmative action? The union's contract stipulates that none of the three can be ignored, and it seems to indicate that they are of roughly equal importance. Should other considerations be taken into account? Analyze the case until it is RESOLVEDD.

18. A DAMAGING AD OR AN EFFECTIVE MESSAGE?
Should You Use a Positive Role Model to Sell a "Negative" Product?

Your ad agency has been employed by many different companies to sell their products over the years, and none have caused as much controversy internally as this new campaign. As the partner in charge of this new account, you have the final say on what will be sent to the client or whether your company decides to stay on the account. When you originally took on the account, it had all seemed fairly straightforward. There was no way you expected events to unfold as they have.

Beast Malt Liquor, a subsidiary of a large brewery and alcoholic beverage conglomerate, hired your agency to design a new, "hip" ad campaign to be aired on networks and billboards in various minority neighborhoods. They said they wanted their message aimed at young inner-city blacks, considered to be their most important customers for various reasons. The main reasons are that this market population has consistently purchased Beast Malt Liquor for years, its consumption is continuing to grow, and there is great room for further growth.

The representative from Beast gave very explicit instructions to your agency as to the thrust of the campaign. You were to aim the ads at young inner-city blacks and especially at upwardly mobile professionals in the black community. The ads had to be tailored to two different income groups, those who had already "made it" and those who were hoping to do so but were still locked into lower-income jobs. Beast's representative said they knew this was a tough goal but that your company was chosen for its innovative techniques. The appeal should give a modern, "hip," "upscale" look to the malt liquor as a way of "upgrading the image" of malt liquor. The representative had said, "Try to make us look sophisticated. We want to be the malt liquor that the wine and cheese crowd would accept. But don't forget our loyal lower-income customers, either."

This had indeed been a challenging task. The creative department had worked long and hard on the theme for the campaign, as well as the first set of commercials and billboards that would be shown to Beast's account executives. The initial product seemed to have everything the client wanted. The first thirty-second film showed a black man dressed in a shirt and tie against the background of a rather bleak inner-city neighborhood. He is, as one of your writers put it, "sitting on the front porch with one of his old homies, sipping Beast Malt Liquor and passing on some good advice." The well-dressed man is telling his pal, who looks barely out of his teens at best, the story of how he got out of the projects and became the first member of his family to go to college. He tells his young friend that college was "cool" and that the education he got now lets him do good things for the old neighborhood. The dialogue plays on the fact that the man sees himself as a role model for his "brothers and sisters who want to break out of the 'hood just like I did." He hopes they can see how good life can be and will follow his lead by going to college.

Initially you had thought, "A stroke of genius!" It's got the upscale image, an appeal to upwardly mobile black consumers, yet includes the old lower-income market segment in the image. Then, too, it appeals to the older age group while including the younger consumers whom Beast wants to capture. And the message is very "upbeat and positive," as one writer had put it. What could be wrong? You soon found out.

When the ad was test-marketed in five or six selected cities, there was a good deal of positive feedback but also a great many negative reactions. Some of the negative criticisms were aimed at the very idea of marketing a high-alcohol content malt liquor at the youth market. This response was, as one of your creative people said, "to be expected whenever you market alcohol products of any sort using young actors." You believe that this is probably true. If this were the only criticism, your company could probably write it off as a generic antialcohol comment. It isn't the only, or even the main, criticism of the ad, however.

Many of the critics in the test markets said the whole commercial was in poor taste. The ad depicts a positive role model on a mission to show that education is good and can put your life on the right track. Nothing wrong there, the critics said, until you realize that the ad loses all its credibility by the role model's "guzzling a malt liquor" as he delivers it. In addition, many of the critics pointed to the fact that the messages in the ad, the education message and the malt liquor message, are aimed at a teenager. One comment said it looked as if the "home boy" was doing the safe thing by sitting on his porch and drinking malt liquor instead of "being out on the street gang-banging." Doesn't this look as if the ad is saying that sitting on a porch drinking liquor is a reasonable alternative to other dangerous activities? This was certainly a mixed message, to be sure.

A second set of criticisms questioned the misleading nature of the ad. They felt that it did no better than earlier commercials relating drinking with romantic, social, and financial success. "This is just the same old story—drink our stuff and the babes and money will come to you" was the way one woman had put it. Drinkers show class and succeed. Do nondrinkers lack class and fail? A number of comments had made this same point. Was the viewer supposed to see that the way to bond with other people or to act as a mentor was through liquor?

Other comments were even more serious. One criticized what looked to be a paternalistic and racist attitude in the commercial. The targeting of urban blacks and other minorities is clearly wrong, given that statistics show this group suffers more than any other from alcohol-related diseases and poor health care. To trade on such a group seemed racist to many critics. Others noted that a liquor company trying to tell people how to live their lives seemed very paternalistic, as if the makers of liquor had "gathered the wisdom of the ages while brewing booze." How patronizing!

You were stunned by the number and ferocity of the criticisms. Could you have so misread the ad when you saw it? Or were these criticisms just the latest statement of the overly sensitive "victim mentality"? Some of the people you had working on the account agreed with the critics and thought maybe the firm should back off the account. They said they personally had never thought about the effects of such advertising, but the critics had opened their eyes. Your creative department was equally shocked. They believed that they were merely trying to show the values and concerns of inner-city consumers. The background images that concerned some critics were not intentionally included but just showed up on the film. Finally, they assure you that everyone in the film is at least twenty-five years old and that there are no underlying, "hidden" messages. In short, they think the criticisms are unjust.

After recovering from your initial shock, you began to analyze the situation. You could send the client the ad, along with the marketing studies. They might reject it or accept it. The problem is that if they accept it and the critics do represent the reaction of the public to the ads, the client suffers, your company suffers, and you personally may be put in a position of having to defend ads that already have been called racist and exploitative. Citizen groups, especially within the black community, might even file lawsuits. Could your firm and the client be branded as racists? These are all consequences everyone would like to avoid. But is it part of your job to protect the client against such negative reactions?

But if you withhold the ad from the client and they find out, you could suffer a loss of the account and the financial effects of that. This could be a multimillion-dollar account. Besides, you have a very good idea that the client would like the ads, so should you worry about the consequences? Isn't your job to give the client what they want? Could your creative department come up with a whole new approach as quickly as necessary? There are deadlines coming up soon. Too soon, in fact, to even reshoot or severely edit the present ads before having to let the client into the discussion. Maybe you should consider just living with the consequences.

As you talked this over with your staff, one member did raise the question of what happens if the critics are indeed correct. That is, what if the ads are exploitative, will convince young people to drink, do portray drinking as much too glamorous, and are racist, at least to many people? Is this possibly going to affect your company's reputation negatively? Are the images and message of the ads harmful, misleading, and an example of using any approach that will sell the product? If so, do you personally want to be associated with them? Does your company? Does this matter, though, if the client is satisfied? Isn't the real moral choice the client's and not yours?

What does seem clear, though, is that some of your own people are convinced that taking the account is a very bad idea. A couple have even said they would not work on the account in the future regardless of whether you decide the company should continue with it. They say they would have to resign unless transferred to other accounts. You don't want to lose these valued employees. But aren't they maybe overreacting a bit? Shouldn't they realize that there are always people ready to object to any liquor sales? If the product is legal and the ads done according to all network guidelines, which this one is, isn't it ethical to take the account?

Many issues need to be RESOLVEDD here, both for you personally and as the account executive. What should you do about this already expensive ad proposal and why?

19. Is This Doctor Sick?
AIDS Testing for Doctors, Honesty, and Personal Loyalty

You could not believe it when your brother, Carl, told you that he had just been tested HIV-positive. You knew, of course, that Carl was gay. But you thought that because he was a doctor, he would have little chance of becoming infected with the AIDS virus. Carl had tried to ease your fears with the information that ongoing studies of HIV-infected people indicated that, with the new drugs on the market now, there is about a 1 in 3 chance that they would actually contract full-blown AIDS. You had read, though, that the studies were far from complete and that some experts maintain that most HIV-infected persons would get AIDS.

This was a long-term worry. However, you face a more immediate problem. You work in Carl's office as the office manager. Twelve people, including two other doctors, four nurses, two receptionists, and two X-ray technicians, also work there. The problem is that Carl asked you not to tell anyone at the office of his test results. "We especially can't let the patients find out," he said.

"But Carl, the AMA [American Medical Association] has required HIV-infected doctors to disclose their condition," you protested.

"Not quite. What the AMA says is that it is unethical for a guy like me not to inform his patients of his condition. Well, ethics cuts two ways here. The AMA is just reacting to AIDS fears and antigay sentiments in the country. Other conditions, even those that are highly infectious, do not require disclosure. What does that tell you? Then there's my privacy. This information is between me and my doctor. My medical history is my private business just as much as my sexual preference," Carl answered.

"That's true, but AIDS is all-consuming and still essentially fatal. What about 'Do no harm'? Isn't that one of the primary ethical obligations of a physician?"

"First," he replied, "I haven't got AIDS. Second, there's a chance I'll never develop it. Third, I'm an internist, not a surgeon. Even if I were, the statistics indicate that the chances of a patient getting infected during surgery are about 0.0065 in a million. Not exactly a high risk, even in surgery. Imagine how low the risk is for non-surgical contacts," Carl said, rather angrily. "Besides, I'm asking you, as my brother, to keep this confidential. Believe me, when I feel it's a significant danger, I'll tell every patient we have."

"That makes it a bit tough on me, Carl. I am the office manager, remember. Don't I have a duty to tell the rest of the staff? At least they should know."

"And if they blurt it out to a patient? Do you know how many ridiculous lawsuits we'd get from patients who have a cold and are convinced it's AIDS? Not to mention former patients who haven't seen me in years and who come down with something, even test HIV-positive for reasons totally unconnected with us? I've told you because I trust you. Let's just keep this in the family."

For all the reasons you had mentioned, you are deeply concerned about your brother's request. Then again, Carl is right about the nature of the minuscule risks involved. The AMA's position is probably overly conservative and may well be formulated just to promote the public image of the profession. Moreover, the AMA has no legal control over a doctor. Many doctors do not belong to the AMA, which is a voluntary professional organization. Finally, there are no federal or state laws requiring it. In fact, in many states laws prohibit a person from disclosing someone's HIV status to a third party, though your state is not one of these. But even if it were, you still couldn't shake the feeling that this is a fact that patients have a right to know and make up their own minds about.

In reviewing some literature on HIV and AIDS, you find that Carl's estimates of the chances of getting infected from a doctor are correct, and maybe even too high. The chances may be as little as 0.00065 in a million for surgical patients. The chances must be even more astronomical for noninvasive procedures. Carl does perform some minor outpatient surgery in the office, but that treatment rarely entails more than removing stitches and lancing boils. The statistics indicate, however, that only between 0.3 and 3 patients in a thousand whose blood mingles with the blood of a surgeon will contact AIDS. These are very long odds.

So, you wonder, if the chances of Carl infecting a patient are so low, shouldn't I honor his request? He is my brother, and he did tell me about this as his brother, not doctor to office manager. Family loyalty is a precious commodity. But so is patient trust. You talk to dozens of patients a week who trust you, Carl, and the whole practice to do their very best for them. Don't you owe them something? If only this AIDS epidemic were not such a political football. There is too much misunderstanding and hysteria involved, so maybe Carl is right. But this is not merely a political decision, for lives are involved.

You wonder whether your worries will ever be RESOLVEDD and the basis of your decision clarified. But you must decide and then live with the results.

20. WORTH THE EFFORT? ▰▰▰▰▰▰▰▰▰▰
Handling Sexual Harassment

Violet Spear had done her homework. But then, she felt she had to in order to know whether she should file a grievance against her coworker, Theo Lucasey. Violet did not want to jeopardize her job as a junior marketing executive by appearing to be a "bad sport," "overly sensitive woman," or a "hysterical female." Theo had called her all of these in the last few months when she complained to him about his conduct toward her. As a member of your company's grievance committee, you must review Violet's charges and decide whether Theo is guilty of sexual harassment.

You and the committee first looked to the legal guidelines on sexual harassment as part of your procedure. Under Title VII of the 1964 Civil Rights Act, sexual harassment is defined as:

> Unwelcome sexual advances, requests for sexual favors, and other verbal or physical conduct of a sexual nature constitute sexual harassment when (1) submission to such conduct is made either explicitly or implicitly a term or condition of an individual's employment, (2) submission to or rejection of such conduct by an individual is used as the basis for employment decisions affecting such individual, or (3) such conduct has the purpose or effect of unreasonably interfering with an individual's work performance or creating an intimidating, hostile, or offensive working environment.[*]

Although the definition was clear to you and the committee, complications arose in the case of Violet and Theo that made the decision tricky.

Violet had been successful in her marketing position. She attributed part of her success to the fact that her clients trust her professionalism, as well as her knowledge of her job. Part of what Violet sees as important to her professional image is her wardrobe: she dresses in very conservative business suits that are feminine, yet reassuring to her conservative male clients. Prior to Theo's remarks, no one had ever referred to her wardrobe as anything but tasteful or stylish.

Theo was transferred from a regional branch about six months earlier and almost immediately began to make comments to Violet whenever they worked together. At first it had just been things like "Very nice suit," but soon he began to add a growl or a low barking noise to his comments. She had called him on this right away, but he accused her of being overly sensitive. The comments continued and gradually became more suggestive. Again Violet told him to keep his comments to himself. He responded by accusing her of being a bad sport.

The situation reached its peak, she alleged, when once again Theo had made a comment about her clothes: "That suit is so sexy I can't stand it. Why don't we go into my office where you can take it off so I can get some work done? You know what kind of work I mean, right?" Violet then replied angrily, "Why don't you just knock it off? Act like a grown man instead of a fourteen-year-old kid with a hormone problem. I simply will not tolerate these remarks anymore. One more and I'm going to have to file a complaint." She felt that she had made it very clear to Theo that she felt harassed and would file a formal grievance if he continued with his remarks.

But—and Theo does not disagree with Violet's report of the facts—he had replied, "Don't be a hysterical female, dear. Those business suits of yours really turn me on. I've always had a thing for women who dress in those 'power suits.' I like power. Why not just stop wearing those clothes? Maybe then I'll be able to control myself." Theo argues, though, that he was merely flirting and teasing a coworker. If he were Violet's boss, he says, this would be different and could be seen as harassment. However, he believes that there was nothing going on that could be called harassment, though perhaps he had teased a bit too hard.

Violet had walked away in disgust and began her research into sexual harassment. In the next week she looked up the harassment guidelines and talked to a number of women at her office about what had happened. When she asked what to do, she

---

[*]*Guidelines on Discrimination on the Basis of Sex* (Washington, D.C.: Equal Opportunity Commission, November 10, 1980).

received replies that were not encouraging, she told the committee. One woman said it couldn't be harassment because Theo wasn't her boss and had no power over her. Another said that she had no confidence that any of the male executives would take her complaints seriously. She even thought that some might make sure the complaint never reached the committee. A third said that unless one of the male executives actually witnessed the harassment, nothing would be done. In all, five different women expressed the sentiment that no male executive would take her seriously and that they would probably believe Theo's comment about her being overly sensitive or hysterical.

"It's the way men are. Must be genetic. No government guidelines are going to reverse forty-one thousand years of habit," one had said.

Violet felt a little betrayed by the company and comments, but the terms of the guidelines seemed to cover Theo's actions: the environment had become oppressive. Yet, she had gotten no encouragement from other women at the company. She had also come across some statistics that stated that 67 percent of the women who complained of harassment lost their jobs within one year, either by being fired or by voluntarily leaving. The same source stated that only 9 percent of the complaints ever resulted in the end of the harassment.

Despite the lack of support by her coworkers, the bad news, and opposition, Violet had gone ahead and carried through the step-by-step procedure for sexual harassment claims at your firm. The result was much as predicted: the male executives she approached tried to smoothe over the whole thing and had no interest in any formal action. One suggested that he meet with her and Theo to mediate. Another suggested she consider requesting a transfer. Such responses made her more and more angry as she moved up the ladder. Now she had filed a grievance and was presenting her case to the grievance committee.

Violet testified that she is afraid of being labeled a complainer or a troublemaker. She also admitted that she had even wondered whether Theo's comments might be correct: maybe if she just stopped wearing those suits he'd leave her alone. She didn't want to compromise her career because she had worked too hard and had done too well to give it up for the antics of a jerk like Theo. Her clients responded well to her professional style of dress and had never insulted her like Theo. Would they be bothered by a switch in her wardrobe? Yet if she didn't complain, work would continue to be oppressive, and there was no telling how many other women Theo would insult.

During his interview with the committee, Theo continued to argue that he had not intended to harass Violet. He thought that she was truly being oversensitive and that a little teasing or flirting should not be considered a serious offense. He is aware that he can be suspended or even terminated if the committee finds against him. In fact, if the committee agrees with Violet, she could file a legal suit against him as well. He had commented that these consequences are far in excess of what might be considered fair. If he had power over Violet or if he had intended to harass her, he might be guilty of harassment. But he pointed out that one cannot harass someone unintentionally.

When you put yourself in Violet's position, you can understand her annoyance. However, when you think of yourself in Theo's position, you can see how he fears being treated too harshly. Some committee members agree that Theo's actions are immature and that Violet has every right to be annoyed, but they do not think that he should be punished by suspension or loss of a job for such comments. They believe that even if he is wrong about Violet being overly sensitive, he did not really intend to create a hostile environment and therefore should not be punished for something he did not intend. Other members of the committee are firmly on Violet's side, saying that harassment is in the eyes of the beholder, not the harasser. Violet's repeated requests that Theo stop constituted fair warning and should have made it clear that his actions were harassment, whether he saw them as such or not. Therefore, he should be punished according to the company's guidelines, which provide for either termination or a suspension without pay for a period to be determined by the committee, along with a record to be included permanently in his personnel file. They do not think that opening Theo to further legal action by Violet is a consideration on which they should base their votes. Those committee members who disagree say that Violet had not been harmed, merely annoyed, and should not be set up to bring even more serious legal actions against Theo.

Your vote is obviously going to be crucial given the split on the committee. The issues do raise significant questions. Can you be fair to both Theo and Violet? You consider justice an important consideration and are worried that either decision can easily be construed to be unfair, whether to Violet or Theo. Moreover, the company's guidelines do leave a lot up to the committee. Is there an appropriate length of suspension? If so, does Theo deserve one? Or does he deserve more severe punishment? How will Violet feel about the company and her job if nothing is done? Will she pursue legal action? Could ignoring Theo's actions make the female employees even more cynical and certain that the company will not take them seriously? Why have a sexual harassment procedure if the company isn't willing to enforce it when a complaint is made? Could the company be sued by Theo if you rule for Violet or by Violet if nothing is done? All of these are important considerations that you must get RESOLVEDD personally and then communicate to the committee.

21. Is Nothing Private?
Using Computers to Obtain Advertising Information

After leaving your boss's office, you were feeling both complimented and confused. He had complimented you by telling you that the assignment he was offering you was based on the fact that you were not only a good advertising agent but also the most skilled worker he had when it came to using the computer. But you were confused about whether to take on the assignment he had offered you. It just seemed to push the limits of privacy and sensitivity a little too far. Then again, there was nothing illegal about what he was asking you to do, and he was therefore expecting you to complete the assignment. This was a tough decision.

The advertising agency you work for had just taken on a new and very lucrative account with a company called FatAway, Inc. This company specialized in a new, very expensive dieting plan, complete with its own food supplements, diet aids, and medical advisory board for its users. As far as you could tell, the products being offered were safe and worked for many people. It wasn't the product that bothered you, however. It was the advertising ploy they asked your company to initiate that was raising questions in your mind.

FatAway's president, Monique Masters, had conceived of a plan to gain national attention for her company. She expects your company, as the ad agency handling her account, to follow through on her "brilliant idea." The idea occurred to her as she was reading a newspaper article called "How Fat Are Americans?" This article had mentioned statistics that ranked states by how much the average citizen exceeded the recommended weight for his or her height. She thought about these statistics, checked with people who knew something about databases and access to them, and concocted her advertising plan. What she wanted to do was to use public information from databases of all the departments of motor vehicles across the country to identify the "ten fattest people in each state." Then FatAway would take out a national ad in newspapers such as *USA Today* naming those 500 people and offering them a free membership in FatAway's program. FatAway would also pay the people $10 a pound for every pound they lost, use them in their literature and future ads, and even pay them a salary as spokespersons for their product if they wished. All this was contingent on the people accepting the offer and actually losing significant amounts of weight.

"This is just the kind of national campaign that can make us the best-known dieting company in the United States," Monique had gushed to your boss. "And you folks can find the information, design the ads, market the campaign, and reap a huge profit from us if it succeeds."

The boss had fallen for the idea hook, line, and sinker. Given your abilities, especially with the computer, he had called you in and offered you the assignment. What you would have to do to begin would be to find a way of accessing all fifty motor vehicle databases. If they could not be easily accessed by computer, you could perhaps find unconventional ways of accessing them or, as a last resort, purchase them from the individual states. He also explained that most secretaries of state sell such lists for modest sums to all sorts of marketing firms, so they are obviously not confidential or private. In fact, he was pretty sure that many states' databases were open to access from anyone who subscribed to particular database services. Your company, as an ad agency, subscribed to almost every major service of this sort. Thus, he said, you should be able to access whatever information the states made available legally.

His next comment started you thinking about the ramifications of this information search. He had added that if you could get "deeper into the databases," you could find out the height and weight of all the people in each state who held driver's licenses. It would then be a time-consuming but simple matter to look for people who were grossly overweight for their height. Then just narrow down the list to ten per state and "we're in business." He also suggested that if you could get into the databases to find the information without having to purchase the lists, which ran a couple of hundred dollars each and might not contain all the necessary information, it would save the company some money. Because the lists were not private, were often sold by states, and contained only information that was a matter of public record, he believed you could complete Monique's assignment and get the campaign off to a roaring start.

Well, you thought, I can probably handle all the computer work and design the national ads for the newspapers, but do I want to do it? Although all the information was public, in a sense wouldn't this be an invasion of people's privacy? That is, when they gave the information to the departments of motor vehicles, they had no idea that it would be used this way. Isn't that a violation of some unspoken agreement? Even if you say it's the states that are violating the trust, is it ethical to reap the benefits of that violation? Then there is the question of publicly embarrassing 500 people by printing their names in national publications and making it very clear that they are grossly overweight and should do something about it. This seems extremely insensitive regardless of whether you have a right to the information or not.

Upon returning to your office, you used your computer skills to access a number of documents concerning computer ethics. One document that you found very interesting was the "ACM Code of Ethics and Professional Conduct." This was the ethics code designed and adopted by the Executive Council of the Association for Computing Machinery in 1992. Among the twenty-four imperatives listed were the following, which seem to pertain to FatAway's marketing plan:

> *1.2 Avoid harm to others.* This provision includes cautions against undesirable loss of information and also against unintended harm that might follow one's actions. It requires the computing professional to carefully weigh the impact of any actions on "all those affected by decisions made during design and implementation."

> *1.7 Respect the privacy of others.* This provision recognizes the vast potential for information gathering that exists today and warns professionals to restrict gathering of personal information to "only the necessary amount."

> *1.8 Honor confidentiality.* The code states, "The ethical concern is to respect all obligations of confidentiality to employers, clients, and users unless discharged from such obligations by requirements of the law or other principles of this code."

> *3.5 Articulate and support policies that protect the dignity of users and others affected by a computing system.* Here the unintentional or intentional use of computers to demean individuals or groups is forbidden.

Given these aspects of the ACM Code, you developed serious reservations about continuing to work on FatAway's campaign. When you explained your concerns to him, your boss had listened carefully and then described the other side of the issue. He first pointed out the fact that you were not a computer professional in the sense of being a designer of systems, programmer, or any other kind of systems expert. Therefore, the code didn't apply to you. Next he had repeated the claim that states often sold their lists legally, so they must be public information. If that was true, you were not violating privacy and confidentiality. Then he added that because neither the states nor the individuals who were on the list were your clients, you could not possibly be violating their trust by using the information you were to obtain. He finally did admit that there could be some embarrassment for the people on the list but that this might be a motivation for them to try a product that was safe, effective, and ultimately made them healthier. Didn't the good that would be done overshadow the initial embarrassment?

You were now back in your office considering your options. Part of you believes the boss has some good points, but part of you believes the ACM Code should be followed. Although you are not technically a computing professional, that is not the issue. The spirit of the code's guidelines surely apply to anyone who uses computers as part of their profession. Computers are powerful tools that can be used for good or that can cause great harm when misused. Privacy, harm, and confidentiality are the concerns of not just computing professionals but all ethical professionals. Yet there is the fact that using information and databases in this way was perfectly legal. Also, as an advertising professional, you have to admit that Monique's idea would grab about as much publicity for her company as any campaign you've ever seen. But would it be productive publicity or a public relations disaster? Ultimately you have to ask yourself what duties you owe to whom. Is your responsibility primarily to your client and company, or do you owe the yet-to-be-named individuals something? Is it acceptable to attack their dignity in this way? Would more good be done or not?

Sitting there you knew these issues must be RESOLVEDD before you could continue with the assignment, if indeed you should continue. Your boss seems to expect you to "do your duty," as he said, but what exactly is your duty? And the real question now is what to do in the circumstances.

22. BRINGING HOME THE WAR ON DRUGS
Should You Inform on Fellow Employees?

As a resident of St. Clinton, a prosperous city of about thirty thousand people located nearly an hour's drive from a metropolitan area, you are one of many civically minded citizens who are involved in all sorts of volunteer work that contributes to maintaining the high quality of life in the area. You and your fellow citizens are proud of your public schools, the many and diverse activities available for people of all ages, and your extensive volunteer services directed to help the needy. For years, you had been proud that the epidemic of illegal drug use that has swept the nation and the business world had largely bypassed your little city.

But just as change is the hallmark of the information age, it is not always change for the better that comes knocking on our doors. A seven-part investigative report last month by the local newspaper, the *Holy Herald,* has shaken the confidence and pride of the town. You and others have been troubled by the extensive reports revealing that drugs are widely used by children in all the schools and that they are readily available in the community.

Just as new problems beget new solutions, the *Herald* has in the past week formulated a seemingly innovative and promising way for ordinary citizens to fight the drug trade. The paper's call to action was accompanied by a coupon with spaces to note the names of drug users and drug dealers and also to report suspicious activity and license plate numbers of cars involved. Citizens are asked to fill out the forms anonymously and turn them in to the newspaper. The editor will forward the completed anonymous forms to the police to spark investigations that should make the drug culture more than unwelcome in St. Clinton.

Although a letter to the editor in a subsequent edition of the paper complained bitterly that such tactics would call forth a kind of witch-hunt, many citizens like the initiative. You have talked to several who argue that the police are powerless against organized crime and that only widespread citizen action can root out the drug menace. Moreover, the accusations will spark investigations, not recrimination of innocent citizens. Only those who are proven to be users and sellers through legal means will be pursued. You, however, are not so sure that this approach is a good idea.

Your objections and those of other opponents are based on your understanding of democracy and individual rights and freedom, as well as awareness of similar tactics used by totalitarian regimes such as Hitler's Nazis and the communists of Stalin and Mao Tse-tung. The civic atmosphere created by citizens who become informants may be like an epidemic, and you suspect that in the end there may be damage to the reputations of innocent people who may have a suspicious appearance such as a long beard or a "spaced-out" personal manner. There are good reasons that ordinary citizens should not seek to become police informants and why police work should be left to the police.

Police investigations are carefully regulated by the legislature and the judiciary branches of government to protect the civil rights of innocent but suspicious citizens. Society has made a major value preference in formulating rules to implement the principle that it is worse for government to harm one innocent citizen than to set free a guilty one. By encouraging citizens to inform on suspicious people and activities, some citizens who are innocent will surely feel the sting of a personal investigation. They in turn will become suspicious of possible informants and thus involved in the spread of suspicion, distrust, and strife.

It is, however, not the newspaper that has raised a problem for you but rather the response of your supervisor at Colossal Health, where you work. She is so enamored of the newspaper's campaign that she called a meeting of you and ten other administrative employees on Monday and told you she expected filled-out copies on her desk by the end of the week. She plans to give them to the newspaper herself, thus providing a second shield of protective anonymity for those who cooperate and turn in leading information.

"This is an idea whose time has come," she said definitively. "We now have an opportunity to show the nation that caring citizens can make all the difference. And besides, just think what this will do for the image of the St. Clinton division of Colossal Health!" Of course, she neglected to point out that she was infringing on the employees' right to privacy. But you know from former experience that she meant what she said, that she would deplore an attempt by her subordinates to dissuade her on the matter, and that she was entirely capable of harassing any who did not comply.

The question at issue is what you should do in the circumstances. You have many choices here and many reasons to favor each. You will need to sort them out and analyze the options if you are to avoid some serious pitfalls and thorny complications in getting it all RESOLVEDD.

23. TWO MINUTES TOO LATE TO HELP? ▬▬▬▬
Is Your Coworker Being Fairly Treated?

"All that for two minutes?" you thought. It did not seem fair to you, and you could tell that it did not seem fair to the other three secretaries who shared your area. Lashondra had arrived at work two minutes late this morning, and her boss, Kendra Carroll, was waiting at her desk when she came in. You and the other secretaries knew this was going to be trouble. You had seen it before. Lashondra had not, because she had been working in your area for only two weeks following her transfer. Surely, she had not confronted this kind of hassle working for Tom Dryden in the downstairs office.

Kendra shouted, "We don't pay you for not being here! Tom Dryden might have, but I won't."

Lashondra didn't have time to say anything before Kendra dropped the largest stack of file folders you had ever seen onto her desk. "Finish typing the cover letters for all of these by noon or else," Kendra snarled. "And I don't want any of the rest of you to touch a single folder, type a single letter, or help this slacker in any way, or you'll have twice as much work to do as she does." The door slammed as Kendra went back into her office.

The look on Lashondra's face was a mix of astonishment and deep anguish. There was no way to do all that work in just three hours. You and the other secretaries tried to console her. But when she asked whether Kendra meant no one could help, no one said anything. You knew she had meant it. But at the same time, you knew Kendra well enough to know she probably would not emerge from her office until the end of the day. She had blown up like this many times before and always seemed to hide in her office the rest of the day, perhaps out of embarrassment.

As Lashondra started in on the files, the others returned to their own work. You, however, just could not concentrate, feeling there must be some way to help. You had no pressing jobs that morning and were, in fact, well ahead of schedule. Indeed, you had been more or less just looking for something to do for the last two days. Shouldn't you pitch in and help Lashondra?

Pat Tashiaki saw you staring at Lashondra. "Don't do it. You know how Kendra acts when people disobey her orders. You'll never have any peace again if you help."

"But Pat, it wasn't fair. She didn't give Lashondra any chance to explain. And two minutes . . . two minutes! Give me a break," you replied.

"Who said life, or Kendra, had to be fair? Remember last year when Neil tried to help me after one of Kendra's tirades? She practically bit his head off. Then for a month, she made his life miserable until he quit. Are you up for job hunting?" Pat warned.

"She'll never know. She never comes out of her office after a blow-up like this. If we all take one file, . . ." You didn't get a chance to finish.

"No way!" was the response from the other three secretaries.

"Please, I need help," Lashondra said. "I need this job. I don't know why Kendra is so tough on me, but for two weeks she's given me a hard time. Maybe because we're both black and she is afraid people will think black women can't hack it in a big corporation. I don't know. But please, help me. This isn't fair. None of you could do all this work by yourself." Lashondra was practically crying.

"Sorry. Can't do it. We need our jobs, too," Pat answered. The others agreed.

You had not replied yet but were thinking hard about your options. It seemed quite possible that you could help without Kendra finding out, unless one of the others told her. But the two of you still might not complete the work.

Maybe you could talk to some higher manager about Kendra and her temper. However, there are no formal procedures for filing a grievance in this company and no union or collective bargaining agreement with any protections for the secretaries. As the tiff between Kendra and Neil proved last year, secretaries are at the mercy of their bosses in this company.

On the other hand, there is a well-known and much publicized corporate ethics policy that offers protection for anyone who files a complaint about possible unethical practices. Kendra's brand of threats and abuse might well be considered unethical conduct. But, of course, you would have Kendra as an enemy for life if you took that route!

On the other hand, why do you feel so sure that Pat is not right in her view that the problem is solely Lashondra and Kendra's to settle? Is there really any ethical or other good reason that you should get involved? And doesn't Kendra have a right to enforce punctuality as a requirement of the job? It should bring you some real peace of mind to have this case RESOLVEDD.

24. Employment at Will? Yes. But Is It Fair?
Was Termination Justified?

You have always had some mixed feelings about working for Jordun Corporation, a small security company, because of their strict policy of employment-at-will. Employment-at-will is the doctrine that employees can be terminated at the discretion of the management, with or without cause. The company policy is based on the idea that the employer owns the jobs it creates, the workplace, the tools, machines and raw materials, and it can do with this private property whatever is allowed by law. So employees are like guests of the company who have no right to a job or continued employment. The company informs all prospective employees of the policy and highlights it at a number of places in the company handbook. It is understood that to accept a job there requires knowing of the employment-at-will policy, so every employee is expected to understand it. The company takes it for granted that accepting a job at Jordun means employees accept the policy.

On the other hand, Jordun has always had a policy of due process for its employees. A grievance and appeals process is in effect, although no one has had to use it since you began working there five years ago. Although you are uncomfortable with the official employment-at-will policy, the company's commitment to due process has given you a feeling of security and justice. And the fact that the policy had not been invoked indicated to you a general harmony among employees. No one had to accept a job there, no one had signed on without being informed of the policy, and no one whom you knew had ever appealed to the grievance committee to contest an unjust termination. So you had few reservations when asked recently to serve on the grievance committee, a standing committee that would only meet if there was in fact a grievance.

This week, however, you have begun to have doubts. For the first time since the company instituted its appeals procedure, someone is using it to protest being fired. Karl K. Klondike had been terminated by the president of the company following a number of complaints by both fellow employees and management officials. Karl's termination stemmed from a series of incidents concerning some of his political and personal views.

The first complaint had been lodged after Karl pasted a large poster on his locker door advertising a lecture by the Grand Duke of the local "skinhead" group. The poster was complete with racial slurs, causing two employees to complain to management. After his immediate supervisor talked to him, Karl removed the poster from the outside of the locker and taped it to the inside. The same two employees complained again, and the supervisor again talked to Karl. Even though he complained that he had a right to free expression, Karl took the poster out of his locker entirely.

Although that could have been the end of it, Karl didn't give up easily. He parked his car in the company lot the next day, having plastered the bumpers and windows with stickers extolling the skinhead group's philosophy in graphic terms. There were offensive slogans and pictures ridiculing a number of ethnic groups and homosexuals. This time three other employees and one midlevel manager had complained to the vice president of the company. The VP directly asked Karl to remove the stickers and to keep his offensive views out of the workplace. Again, Karl claimed that his right to free speech gave him the right to put anything he wanted on his own car. The VP had responded that the parking lot was company property, and the company wanted to avoid offending people. The VP then told Karl that he was banned from using the company parking lot unless he removed his offensive stickers.

Karl, deciding to continue his fight for his rights, now began to park his car on the street directly in front of the entrance to the building where everyone could see it as they came to work every day. Because the street was public property, no one at the company could do anything about the car being there. For a few days, everyone just tried to ignore Karl's car and get on with their jobs. But then the final incident and complaint came in.

While he was on an assignment as a security guard at the local baseball stadium, Karl's car had been spotted in the stadium employee's lot by one of the owners of the team. When he had discovered that it was Karl's car, he told Karl to get it off the stadium lot or else. Karl had complied but made it known that he felt the owner was wrong and violating his civil rights. Although he worked through the ball game that day, he had spent a lot of time grumbling and asking other workers whether they thought he had been treated unfairly. The owner had then called and asked that Karl not be assigned to his stadium ever again.

This time, the president of Jordun Corporation was informed of the situation. He talked with various employees and managers about Karl's views and the previous incidents before deciding to terminate Karl. He gave Karl one week's notice as required by the termination policy. During that week, Karl filed an appeal to your committee, claiming that he was being unfairly terminated. His main argument was that no one, not even the stadium owner, had ever complained about how he performed his job. He said that until he tried to express his personal beliefs, he had never gotten anything but good performance reviews. He also pointed out that he had never been late for work, never missed an assignment, and had never even taken a sick day in almost two years of working for Jordun.

When Mr. Scott, the president, appeared before your committee, he did not dispute any of Karl's claims about his job performance. He did, however, point out that there had been a client complaint and a number of complaints from other workers and two managers. Although none of the complaints involved bad job performance, morale and the company's image had surely suffered. Therefore, he had invoked the employment-at-will doctrine in terminating Karl. And now that he had made his decision, it did not matter why Karl was being fired, Scott said. As president, he no longer wanted Karl working for Jordun Corporation. Just cause was not required.

Karl had then addressed the committee, saying that employment-at-will was an unfair policy that had been abandoned by many companies over the years for that reason. Moreover, he was being fired for no reason except that he had chosen to exercise his right to free speech. He argued that when asked, he had complied with everyone's requests. He had moved his posters, parked outside the company lot, and had also moved his car from the stadium lot. Did employers have the right to fire someone for their political views even when there were no real problems with that person's job performance? Sure, he knew of the employment-at-will policy at Jordun but had thought that it would never be invoked unfairly and in violation of an employee's civil rights. Finally, he asked whether such an unfair policy took precedence over the U.S. Constitution and its guaranteed right to free speech.

After hearing all the facts, you had to wonder about Karl's final question. It seemed to you that Karl had not violated any company policies. He had always performed his job satisfactorily. He indeed had complied with all the requests concerning his poster or stickers. And, you thought, it does appear that he was fired for his personal beliefs rather than a job-related error. Can the fact that Karl's beliefs appear racist and disgusting to management and many employees justify his firing?

There is, however, the employment-at-will clause in the company's policy handbook. Strictly speaking, any reason is enough reason for termination. Yet, why have an appeals policy and Grievance Committee if that is all there is to it? Doesn't having such a committee imply that some firings could be unfair? If not, then at least it must indicate that management has some concern about employee rights or due process. Are these contradictory policies?

Does the company's right to do as it pleases with its private property outweigh Karl's right to free speech? He must have known his views would be offensive to someone, so was he trying to upset his coworkers? Does such a consideration even make a difference? Could it be fair to fire someone for non-work-related factors? Or were the complaints of other employees and one client enough to constitute just cause? In fact, they had complained of nothing but Karl's expression of his personal beliefs.

Whether or not this is a contradictory policy, the employment-at-will policy is in the handbook. Karl knew about it when he brought his personal views to work. There is also the important question of whether the employment-at-will doctrine itself is ethical. If not, how can it justify Karl's termination? But isn't the company entitled to follow a stated and known policy? All these questions are important to you as you decide whether to uphold Karl's termination. One vote might make a difference here, and you are glad that all votes will be cast by secret ballot. There is much to be RESOLVEDD before you cast your vote.

25. PADDING OR PROFIT?
Are You Willing to Pad a Sales Price?

This was your first business trip. Having worked as a sales trainee for six weeks, your supervisor felt it was time to send you along with one of the company's best salesman to observe his handling of customers. Vince Collier was generally referred to in tones of respect and wonder at the office; he had been the company's number one sales rep for five years running. If you were ever going to learn the secrets of good sales techniques, it would be on this trip with Vince.

On Sunday evening you met Vince at the airport and boarded the plane bound for Cincinnati. On the flight, Vince told you a little about his start in sales with the company, while you told him how this was your first sales job and you wanted to learn how to be successful.

"A real go-getter, eh? Well, I can see that I've got a willing student here. Don't worry, kid, I'll show you the ropes," Vince said.

On Monday morning you accompanied Vince on two different calls and observed him in action. He was very good, but he told you these first two calls were the easy ones because he had been dealing with these companies for years. The next was where your education would begin. After months of persistent calling, Herb Norton of Apex Corporation had agreed to let Vince explain your company's product line. He explained that he had been happy with his previous suppliers until recently. They had become more difficult to deal with, so he was looking around for new options.

"Herb's a hard sell, but I think we can get him to throw some business our way," Vince told you as you entered Apex's front door. It turned out to be no exaggeration.

Every time it looked like he was going to agree to make a purchase, he'd pull back. However, Vince was up to the task and kept plugging away until it looked like this was it. But there was one more hitch.

"Look, Vince, I'll be honest," Herb began, "I had a pretty good deal going with my old suppliers until they had a big turnover last month."

"Well, you'll get a good deal from us," Vince answered.

"That remains to be seen. Suppose I lay it out for you? Your prices are a little high, though I believe you when you say the quality is worth the extra cost. But how about this? Suppose I agree to pay you 1 percent more than you're asking?" Herb leaned back in his chair to watch your expressions. You noticed at once a change in the expression on Vince's face.

"What do you mean, Herb?" Vince asked.

Herb then asked Vince whether you could be trusted, and Vince said you could. He explained that you were a real go-getter who was willing to do whatever it took to get a sale.

"Well, it would work like the deal I had with our previous suppliers. What I mean is, I'll authorize our company to pay the higher price, but you report the lower price to yours. We now have a 1 percent surplus to play around with. You take half of that and I'll take the other half. I figure with our volume, we'll each make about $5,000 a year clear and free. You can split yours with the kid any way you want. All you have to do is write up two order forms: one for my people with the higher price, one for yours with the lower. No one will know except us."

Vince said he'd like to think about the offer overnight and talk it over with you. After his last call tomorrow, he would call Herb with the answer.

That night Vince and you discussed Herb's offer. You told him you were absolutely against it. But Vince said you ought to consider all the angles. He told you that this sort of thing was not at all uncommon and that it would not hurt the company. You would be getting the right price for your materials, so the company would make its usual profit. And a little extra cash would come in handy for both of you.

When you objected that the deal was illegal, Vince countered that because no one could find out, there was nothing to worry about. And if questions arose, you could say it was Herb's scam and you didn't know he was doing it. If Herb got caught, you could deny having written up two order forms because they were typed and couldn't be traced back to either of you.

To all of your objections Vince had smooth and rehearsed answers. He was a powerful salesman yet was unable to allay all of your doubts.

"Look, we get paid to bring in sales. I bring in $400,000 of business every year, and our company loses nothing. You said you'd do anything it took to be successful. Well, did you mean it? I've had similar arrangements in the past and they worked out well for everyone." Vince explained that a 1 percent markup would not hurt Herb's company, especially because your product was worth at least that much more.

And then as you left to return to your room, you told Vince that you would sleep on it and let him know in the morning. But now, in the darkness of the night, questions keep running through your mind that Vince had not answered. The ethical ones seem the most troubling and important.

Sure, the economics seemed right, but isn't honesty worth more than the money? You could just refuse to participate and let Vince and Herb do whatever they wanted. But aren't there ethical principles that require you to report Vince to the company if you think he is doing something wrong? Or is it best for you just to forget it, because Vince is so well respected and successful? It is obvious he has done this sort of thing before. Maybe such deals are the key to success in sales. Perhaps the company knows or suspects that Vince has been pulling things like this all along and really does not care as long as he brings in big contracts. Would you be seen as naive, a crybaby, jealous, disloyal, or not a team player if you reported Vince? And if you did so, what good would it do you and your career in the end? You must develop careful answers to all these questions before morning to have the problem RE-SOLVEDD as you promised.

26. LANGUAGE POLICE
IN THE WORKPLACE?
Dealing with a Bilingual Workforce

Being the owner of your own business had been everything you thought it was going to be, both the good and some of the bad. But you are now facing a serious morale problem and ethical conflict involving your workers on the loading dock. You employ nine workers in the loading dock area, including the supervisor. Seven of the workers and the supervisor are from Mexico and the other worker is Puerto Rican. All nine speak both Spanish and English, though not all speak fluent English. As a result, most of the work-related conversation in the loading dock area is conducted in Spanish. This is the source of the problem you face.

Because of the location of the dock area, almost every worker entering the plant has to pass through it a number of times a day on their way in, out, to and from lunch, and to the locker room. It is not uncommon that workers overhear the Spanish conversations as they pass. The vast majority of these workers speak English but no Spanish whatsoever. On a number of occasions in recent weeks, English-speaking workers had heard comments in Spanish that seemed to be directed at them only to be followed by laughter from the other Spanish-speaking workers. Whether it was because a joke had been made at the expense of the English-speaking workers was not clear to you, but these workers had begun to believe the Spanish speakers were making fun of them.

Over the course of a few weeks, the situation had escalated to the point where the English-speaking workers had begun to loudly question the Spanish speakers, asking, "What are you saying? Can't you speak English?" Twice, when no English explanation followed, the English-speaking workers had yelled, "We're in America—speak the language we speak or go back to Mexico." Finally, a near-fight had occurred, which prompted the English-speaking workers to come to you and complain about the situation.

After saying they were sick of being laughed at and ridiculed every time they passed through the dock area, they asked you to institute an English-only policy at the company. They argued that a number of nearby states had passed laws making English the official language for conducting most state business. They also pointed out that many local county and city governments in your state were considering adopting such policies. Because the morale of the English-speaking workers was being seriously undermined, a policy seemed to be the solution. Moreover, the English-speaking workers said that there had been problems with on-the-job communication because they could not understand the dock workers, who tended to begin every conversation in Spanish. They contended that time was lost and efficiency compromised because of the "bilingual shop" you had allowed to develop in the plant.

When you had spoken to the dock supervisor, he tried to explain that it was difficult for some of his workers to switch to English, even when they were dealing with non-Spanish speakers. They felt very uncomfortable with English, spoke Spanish at home and in their neighborhoods, and were afraid of being made fun of when they misspoke at work. He said that a number of such incidents had occurred, although, until the last few weeks, none had occurred for more than a year. But he did say that he understood how the English-speaking workers felt about the situation and would try to get his people to be more careful to avoid offending anyone. He acknowledged that his workers had made some jokes in Spanish, but he also said that they were in no way serious or offensive. His workers were really just nervous, and the jokes had helped them cope with feeling out of place in an English-speaking country.

As a result of these talks, you brought the leaders of the two groups together to try to establish an understanding. However, very little compromise seemed likely. The spokesman for the English speakers demanded an English-only policy. The dock supervisor responded by saying that such a policy would be insulting to his workers and himself. Additionally, he said he had thought America was a "diverse society" and could tolerate a little linguistic freedom. The morale of the English workers shouldn't suffer that much if his people avoided making any more jokes.

Although this proposal seemed initially reasonable to you, the English-speaking workers were not satisfied. They still contended that jokes and comments about them would go on. Their main argument, however, continued to be that in America, English was the language of business. If workers could not rely on other workers speaking English, the only result would be lower productivity, misunderstandings, and possibly more violent incidents. The English-only policy was the only remedy, they said. If you wouldn't institute such a policy, trouble would follow.

The Spanish-speaking workers repeated their contention that they had a right to speak their own language wherever they wished. America guaranteed free speech, not free English speech only. To be insulted by being forced to speak a language someone else demanded them to speak was something they could not accept. Indeed, a number of them had mentioned quitting if you adopted the English-only policy.

It seemed that whatever remedy you sought would offend one group or the other. The situation was difficult for you in other ways, too. The English-speaking workers tended to be more senior, having been hired ten to twelve years ago when you began the company. The Spanish-speaking workers had been hired more recently, having moved to your area of the country in only the last couple of years. Did you owe more to the workers you had employed for a longer time period? Shouldn't they have a right to feel they were not being ridiculed at work? Or did you owe something to the Spanish-speaking workers who had performed well but tended to have more problems finding jobs in your city, if statistics were any indication? It seemed the Spanish-speaking people would be harmed more if they felt they had to quit or were being driven out by the English-only policy. On the other hand, is there anything to the idea that English should be the "language of business," as the English speakers contended? It is true that English-only policies had been gaining acceptance across the country.

It will not be easy for you to sort out all the issues that could be important. Certainly there did seem to be a right to speak freely in America, even in Spanish. Is there something wrong with compromising that at work? Even if it is legal, other considerations are significant here. Would English only at work be a form of ethnic discrimination? Are the morale and productivity of the English-speaking workers really being negatively affected by the Spanish spoken on the job? You understood how there might be problems from time to time. Maybe efficiency would improve with a single-language policy. It all seems so confusing, especially given the emotional nature of many of the issues for the workers. Did an employer even have the right to demand that workers speak a particular language on the job? Is this a violation of their autonomy and privacy? How can this linguistic dispute be fairly and ethically RESOLVEDD? Will an English-only policy clear it all up?

27. MUST A REPORTER BE A GHOUL?
Journalism, Privacy, and the Public's Right to Know

Although you never thought that you would find the perfect summer job, you had it last summer! You were a summer intern for the local newspaper, the *Ripton Daily Centurion.* Ripton is a town of twelve thousand people, located in the Midwest, and the *Centurion* has a readership of just over fifteen thousand in the three-county area. Surely not the *New York Times,* the *Centurion* is a good small-town paper with a fine record of covering the news, and it has earned some journalism awards to its credit.

Although you had no experience working on school publications, your interest in writing had led you to consider journalism. Your uncle had introduced you to a golf partner who was the editor of the *Centurion.* An interview, examination of your records, and your letters of recommendation had brought you this rich opportunity to experience journalism in action.

Your first few days on the job were filled with basic orientation: meeting people, learning how the paper was put together, and talking to reporters. You were next assigned to accompany Carl Woodside, a veteran award-winning reporter, as he developed the stories on his beat. You worked with Woodside for two weeks, and then moved on to other reporters who covered different areas. Such a variety of experience was to give you a broad view of journalism that would motivate and enrich your studies in journalism school as a freshman at the state university in the fall. In reality, however, it posed for you a dilemma that you did not resolve last summer in your first journalism class and are now going to need to address, which is considering the ethics of reporting the news.

Your stint with Woodside began with two days covering a political rally, a town council meeting, and interviews with three firefighters who had been injured in a fire at a gas station. None of this prepared you for that third day on the beat.

While driving through town midafternoon, you heard a loud crash nearby. Woodside applied the brakes gently as you both turned to look. Woodside yelled, "Oh, my God, an accident!" and swung around to race back to the scene. Three cars were tangled in the middle of an intersection. As soon as Woodside found a place to park, you ran to the scene. Two of the drivers were just crawling out of their cars, shaken and bruised but not seriously injured. The driver of the third car was on the pavement, still on her knees beside the backseat, head in hands, crying and screaming. A quick look, and Woodside sent you back to the car for the camera.

When you returned, he pointed to the backseat where an injured child appeared, about four years old. The woman was apparently the child's mother. She was screaming over and over, "Call an ambulance!" A lady on the lawn of a nearby house yelled that she had done so. You were not prepared, however, for what happened next.

Woodside ordered you to poke your head into the car's open window and take pictures of the injured child. The mother apparently overheard the instruction, yelling at you, "Stay away from him, you ghoul! If you get near him, I'll kill you! Just leave us alone!" At that, she rose and threw herself between you and the car.

Woodside yelled at you, too: "Get the picture! Get it now!"

You hesitated, caught in a conflict of wills.

"What's your problem, can't you do your job? Snap the damn thing!" As he yelled this, Woodside actually tried to pull the woman out of your way.

Quite frantic and even out of breath, Woodside then began firing questions at her. "How did this happen? Whose fault was it?"

You just stood there, confused. As the ambulance arrived, Woodside told you to shoot the transfer of the child to the ambulance. At this point, you managed to carry out your orders. The ambulance whizzed away, and you spent an hour observing Woodside's questioning of the other drivers, witnesses, and police. Then you both headed back to the office to write up the story.

In the car on the way, Woodside lashed out at you. He said that your job was to follow his orders. As a journalist, you had to cover tough stories. The public had a right and a need to see the details of such a nasty accident. Woodside went on and on, making related remarks.

When you protested that the woman had asked you not to take the pictures, Woodside screamed, "What does she care about the public's right to know? It isn't her job to cover the news! But it is ours. Next time, do what I say or quit this job if you can't hack it, kid."

Now these words echoed in your mind, bringing back the shock and anxiety you felt last summer. One question that can be asked in many ways loomed as large now as it did then: What should a reporter do in such a situation? Did Woodside do the right thing? Does the job of a reporter really require one to violate the wishes of a distraught victim, as he thought? Would a reporter be shirking his duty to act in a more restrained and less intrusive manner? You now must consider these questions as a part of your thinking about journalism itself as a major.

It is clear that to address this one big question you will need to formulate a general statement of the duty of a newspaper reporter in a society with freedom of the press. You will need to consider the question of the social benefit of reporting the details of an automobile accident and the obligation to your employer of doing so. You must also consider the question of the rights to privacy of an accident victim. And finally, for this question to be fully RESOLVEDD, you must decide the weight of the personal preferences of the individual who is a reporter.

28. JOB INSULATION ▬▬▬▬▬▬▬▬▬▬▬▬▬▬▬
Health and Safety on the Job

You are being exposed to asbestos every day as a filing clerk at Mainline Construction Company. Mainline's office is located in an old, converted bank building. The files, with which you work every day, are located in two former bank vaults in the basement of the building. You recently discovered that the vault was lined with asbestos-impregnated wallboard, and that the overhead pipes are insulated with asbestos.

As part of the yearly inspection of all businesses, a county inspector cited Mainline for various minor building violations last week. The most serious was the asbestos contamination in the vault. The county gave Mainline nineteen days to clean up the fallen asbestos fibers in the vaults. It also fined Mainline $1,200 for the violations. However, it did not require the company to remove or seal off the asbestos in the wallboard or on the pipes, although it strongly recommended doing so.

The company said that it had complied with the citation by cleaning up the fallen fibers. Beyond that, nothing was planned. A memo from the president's office stated, "Employees would be required to perform their normal job duties, including entering the vaults when necessary." The memo went on to note that no employees would be required to move any boxes or perform any activities that could damage the asbestos or release fibers into the air. It also stated that the county citation did not require the areas to be restricted.

You and the other clerks have been talking about the citation and the hazards of asbestos. One employee, sixty-eight-year-old Rich Potowski, vehemently supported management's memo. In fact, he said that you were all nuts to be worried about this asbestos scare at all.

"You youngsters are all worrying about nothing. If you don't bother the asbestos, it won't bother you. Most of us old guys were educated in schools that used asbestos insulation. Every hot water pipe was covered with the stuff. I don't see any evidence of an epidemic of lung cancer or asbestosis in my old schoolmates," Rich argued, rather angrily.

"But what about all those lawsuits against companies like Johns-Manville? All those people with cancer who worked there?" you asked.

"Hey, listen, those people worked in very confined areas where the air was filled with asbestos so thick you could cut it with a knife. It's no wonder they got problems. We've wasted millions in this country on asbestos cleanup when the safest thing is just to leave it alone or cover it with a good-quality paint—you know, like in the vaults," was Milt's response.

You have heard, on many TV home repair shows, that it is sometimes better and cheaper just to let the stuff sit. The real problems occur when it is moved and particles are released into the air.

"Look, the report said it was dangerous to let us into the vaults. That's the bottom line. Why are they forcing us to go in? I say we refuse," Lara Mayfield exclaimed. "And Rich reminds me of those people who say that if it was OK for their fathers to beat them, it's OK for everyone. I just don't buy it."

"You know how much asbestos removal costs? I would guess about $12,000 for those two vaults downstairs. The company isn't going to do it unless the county makes it," was Rich's last remark as he walked out of the lunchroom.

As it turned out later, Rich was right. The company refuses to do more than the citation demands. This does not include removing the asbestos in the vaults. The president circulated another memo that did little more than restate his earlier one. All of this followed a series of complaints by employees and discussions with management. And now the president has refused to discuss the case any further. You had been present at these meetings, so you knew the president was not about to back down. He continually referred to the fact that a reinspection by the county had verified compliance and that the county was satisfied. Beyond that, he said, the company had no obligations to do more. Once it had met the legal requirements, it had no additional obligations to remove the asbestos.

It seems clear at present that you either have to continue to work in the vault or quit your job. Of course, other options might arise if someone went public with the whole incident. You wonder whether such extreme measures are justified.

The county knew of the problem and cited the company. And now, as Rich and the president say, the company has complied with the citation, at least legally. However, there does seem to be a threat to your health here. Evidence indicates that even one asbestos fiber can become lung cancer, though this may take twenty years or more. Even if the asbestos isn't directly disturbed, won't there always be a few fibers floating around? Shouldn't they all be removed? The company's position is clear on that.

Perhaps going to customers or the general public would pressure the company to remove the asbestos. But such whistle-blowing would surely threaten your job. Even if you can remain anonymous, don't you owe the company more than this? A loyal employee is not one who bad-mouths the company to customers or the public. Think of the harm that could be done to business and everyone working for Mainline. But, then, what of the potential for harm done to those of you who work in the vaults? Does the health risk to a few employees justify harming the whole company?

What should you do? How can you best go about deciding the issue? Is the risk too great, or is Rich right? And if the risk is significant, is whistle-blowing the only choice left? It certainly seems to be at this point. You have no ulterior motive here. You are not a disgruntled employee looking to ruin the company; you are merely someone who believes there is a right to safety in the workplace and that your employer is ignoring it. But another part of you believes that perhaps Rich is right and it is better to leave well enough alone. With whistle-blowing seemingly your only alternative apart from quitting or staying on the job, should you pursue it? Analyze the case until it is RESOLVEDD.

29. REPAIR QUOTAS
When Your Job Conflicts with the Customers' Best Interests

As the repairs manager at a franchised but independently owned auto repair shop, you have been given a monthly volume quota by the owner of the shop. For each thirty-day period that you meet the quota, you are rewarded with a bonus that amounts to 20 percent of your monthly salary of $2,500. This is an important opportunity for you now that you have two daughters and a mortgage. In addition, you tend to view the quota as a test of your skill, giving you a chance to exceed your base salary on a regular basis. If you fail to meet the quota for three consecutive months, however, the owner has made it clear that he would consider hiring a new manager and either letting you go or demoting you to a lesser position with a smaller salary and no bonuses.

For the first four months of your job at the shop, you had no problem meeting the quota. Because it was summer and vacation season, many people brought in their cars for maintenance and repairs prior to leaving on their vacations. Now, in midfall, however, business has started to tail off, and you have barely made your quota for the last two months.

As business continues to decline, it becomes clear that you will have to sell the customers on repairs and parts that are desirable but not urgent. This situation troubles you, as candor and honesty have always been among your highest values. You are also concerned that losing your job or taking a cut in salary may force you to look for a new job in a very tight job market.

Recently, even the mechanics have pressured you to "give the customers the old hard sell" so there would be more work. The mechanics want to put in some overtime before Christmas, and they have even been "coaching" you on how to encourage customers to spring for additional repairs "as a safety precaution." The mechanics also have mentioned that their livelihoods depend on you drumming up some business. You still feel squeamish about trying to pressure customers, and so far you haven't tried very hard to sell optional repairs as if they are more needed and more urgent than is absolutely necessary.

When you talk to the owner about your doubts, he says not to worry. "With a little practice, you will become a pro! After all," he explains, "the repairs are, in reality, preventive maintenance. They'll save the customers money in the long run by helping them avoid costly breakdowns with heavy towing fees." He reminds you that his quota policy is nonnegotiable and that failing to meet it will necessitate evaluating your future at his shop.

Your talks with other employees have convinced you that this policy is the creation of this shop owner. It is not part of the general policy of the corporation that sells the franchise. In addition, you are aware that the company retains considerable control over its franchises, although each is a privately owned shop. From what you gather, a call to the nearest franchise representative might get the company involved and lead to the elimination of the quotas or even the cancellation of the franchise. However, you are unsure of the company position on such issues and hesitate to risk your boss becoming aware of your meddling. If he found out about your effort to restrain his approach to employees and customers, you might lose your job, whether you meet the quotas or not.

Wouldn't it be safest just to go along with your boss's desires? Why not just look at it the way he suggested: as a way of getting the customers to buy preventive maintenance? Is it, after all, unethical to sell safety?

On the other hand, warning your customers of the possibility of a breakdown and their chance to prevent it now can be a kind of scare tactic. After all, breakdowns are always possible. The mere fact that you can tell that a part is, for example, visibly worn is not good justification for telling a customer that a breakdown is possible when you know full well that such parts often go for another fifty thousand miles without trouble. Is there any way to distinguish a warning that is motivated largely by your desire to sell from one motivated by an impartial and objective and responsible finding that prudence and safety require you to inform the customer of a possible accident?

This is clearly a case in which the devil is in the details. That is, examination and interpretation of the likely impacts of each of your main options and the principles at stake in each will reveal the relative positive and negative value of your options. Once you have RESOLVEDD the case, you must act in a way you can take pride in.

30. PIECEWORK OR PEACE? ▬▬▬▬▬▬▬▬▬▬
Coworkers Demand Another Worker's Removal

You have been listening to the union steward for the assembly area, Jasmine Booth, for quite a few minutes about the trouble that is brewing. Four weeks ago the company, an electrical supplies manufacturer, hired a number of college students for the summer. One of them, Paul Monroe, was assigned to Jasmine's area, a diverse shop that completes seven different kinds of assemblies. You remembered Paul from his interview with you, the shop superintendent. He seemed like a good summer worker, and you had liked him. Who knew he'd be the center of a troublesome complaint?

Paul began his job by working at a threading machine. His task was to center a metal cap and washer on the screw threads of an electrical conduit pipe, an insulating pipe through which wires are run. Then he was to hold the cap in place while pushing a pedal with his foot that started the threader turning, thus tightening the cap. It was a job that required practice and concentration. Paul never came close to making the piece rate of 175 per hour. He just didn't have the manual dexterity to thread the caps quickly. During his first week at work, Paul never completed more than seventy-five pieces per hour. In the next two weeks, he worked his way up to about 125. Meanwhile, a number of the women who worked nearby took a liking to him and tried to help him improve at his job. However, he just did not develop the skill needed to earn a bonus. But the women, all in their fifties, encouraged him and treated him as if he were a family friend.

Paul seemed to be a well-liked member of your department until you moved him to a new job during his fourth week. This job required little dexterity but a good deal of muscle. He was to put a metal cover onto the body of a fuse box and pound the cover on a metal block to snap it into place. Paul, a weight lifter, was able to knock the cover into place with one hit. The four women who were doing the same job had to hit the cover three or four times to snap it into place. By the end of his first day, Paul was finishing over 250 fuse boxes an hour, 100 more than the hourly rate set by management.

This was the source of the trouble. Piece rates were set by management in conjunction with the union. Every six months or so, a manager from the main office would come to observe a job, tally the number of pieces completed by three selected workers in an hour, then average their rates, which would then become the hourly standard. If too many people earned bonuses or if one person worked significantly faster than anyone else, management would review the job and raise the standard rate to the number done by the fastest worker. The rate for fuse boxes was 150 an hour. Paul's extraordinary productivity had caught the attention of a number of union workers. Two of them complained to you that Paul was wrecking the rate. They were afraid that some manager would think that it was possible for everyone to do 250 boxes an hour and then raise the rate.

These two women had always exceeded 175 when they were put on this job, thereby making a bonus that amounted to around $40 a week. If the rate went up to 250, they would no longer earn their bonuses. They had demanded that Jasmine advise Paul to slow down his rate. They claimed that as their union steward it was her job to look out for the union members. The women pointed out that Paul was not in the union because he was just summer help.

Jasmine had told the women that she did not think it was fair to prevent Paul from earning a bonus. No one had worried when Paul couldn't make a bonus before. They responded coldly that they did not care, because he would be gone in another month and they would be stuck with the higher rate. She had reassured the women by suggesting that they wait a few days to see if Paul might not slow down some on his own, fatigued by his fast pace.

After hearing Jasmine out, you decided to take a look at the situation for yourself and casually walked around the shop observing Paul. You noticed, over the next day or so, that none of the women would talk to Paul or sit next to him at lunch. Even Martha Lahti, who seemed previously to look out for Paul, stayed away. Paul looked confused and hurt by the situation.

That afternoon, you mentioned the problem to the union vice president, who agreed with the women. The VP simply said that Paul was not your concern but that the raising of the piece rate was union business. It was unreasonable for you to expect women to work as quickly at that job as a nineteen-year-old, 210-pound male. He then told you to either slow Paul down or ask upper management to transfer him out of your area, because no other positions were available in your shop for Paul. Jasmine had clearly explained the situation to the VP, and he had certainly reached his decision quickly. He even blamed Paul for a drop in morale, citing the fact that many of the women seemed to be avoiding him and were obviously angry with him.

While reviewing the situation, a number of questions came to mind. Isn't Paul producing more for the company? Isn't that what everyone was supposed to be doing to increase profits? Weren't you all working for the same thing? Didn't Paul deserve to earn as much as he could honestly manage from his own hard work? After all, he wasn't doing anything wrong. In fact, he was doing too much right. Surely there is some way of addressing this issue that would be fair to Paul, the company, and the union workers. Then again, you are management, so the question of who you owe more to, the company and its profits or the union workers who help produce that profit, is important. Many of these union workers are people you have worked with for years. Yet you feel the union is being very unfair to Paul and may be acting out of pure self-interest. How far they will go to get Paul removed is not clear. Could they begin a work slow down? How will your working relations with the union workers be affected by your decision? Can you look yourself in the mirror and feel good about removing Paul? Does this matter? You will need to consider very carefully the options and the values at stake to see that the situation is justly RESOLVEDD.

31. PERSONAL BELIEFS, PUBLIC POLICY ▰▰▰▰▰
Can a Union Force a Member to Support
Its Political Causes?

You had been serving as the president of the local union for almost five years, after twenty years on the loading dock, when Guido Contralli's appeal came to you. Guido was not a full member of the union but rather paid "compulsory agency fees" that allowed him to work at Cash Standard Motors (CSM), a manufacturer of small engines. CSM operated according to an agreement with the union that sanctioned nonunion workers in certain areas of the plant as long as those workers contributed agency fees to the union.

The union position was that Guido and the other nonunion workers benefit from negotiations conducted by the union, receiving higher pay, more benefits, and better working conditions as a result. Therefore, the union reasoned, he and the others owe something to the union in return. Because CSM is not a closed shop, Guido had not been forced to join the union. The agency fees amounted to two-thirds of regular union dues, which are deducted from workers' paychecks in twelve monthly payments. For years you had thought that this policy was fair, as did those workers who paid the two-thirds fees, because the union had secured for them all the benefits enjoyed by regular union members. The health coverage alone would have cost nonunion members twice as much as normal union dues, so everyone seemed happy with the arrangement, at least until recently.

The problems began when the union, considered liberal in its political leanings, decided to put its influence and financial support behind candidates and organizations campaigning for abortion rights for women. The union subsidized a number of pro-abortion political candidates in the last election, as well as donated a significant amount of money to Planned Parenthood, a group known for its support of abortion rights. In addition, a number of other union officials had spoken out publicly in favor of a woman's right to choose abortion up to the end of the second trimester, the legal cutoff point established by the U.S. Supreme Court's *Roe v. Wade* decision. Guido Contralli had responded last month by canceling payroll's authority to take his monthly deductions for union agency fees. You had talked to him at that time.

It isn't that Guido is opposed to unions or that he does not believe the union has a right to speak out on political or moral issues. His problem is that, as a political conservative and a devout Catholic, he believes that abortion is immoral and ought to be made illegal. As far as he is concerned, abortion is the unjustified taking of a human life for what usually amount to less than compelling reasons. He also agrees with the Catholic Church's official antiabortion position, which holds that having an abortion is a sin. As a result, he has refused to allow any of the money he pays to the union to be used to back causes and actions that he personally believes are immoral and unethical. Originally, you had offered to pay the agency fees to a local charity that secures adoptive parents for unwanted babies. The union refused this offer but did suggest that you cut your agency fees by an amount proportionate to the percentage of its budget that goes to support pro-choice causes. You had refused, saying that any money you paid to the union gave at least tacit support to its liberal stance on abortion.

Last week, CSM's personnel director came to you saying that, with the agreement of the union, they intended to fire Guido on the grounds that the union-management agreement required all nonunion members to pay the appropriate agency fees. It would violate company policy and the union contract to allow him to keep his job. Management and the union should agree, he said, that Guido's continued employment would amount to freeloading on the union. It would cost the company, the union, and union workers money that they had no obligation to provide. They would be supporting the costs of negotiation for you without appropriate compensation. You realized that this was exactly what you and other union leaders had used as an argument when negotiating with management for the present arrangements years before. How could you disagree now?

Guido, on the other hand, believes that this violates Title VII of the 1964 Civil Rights Act, which prohibits firing employees for their deeply held religious beliefs. CSM denies that he is being fired for his beliefs. They argue, rather, that he is being fired for not paying his agency fees, a clear violation of the contract. CSM wants you, as union president, to back them up. Union membership is split on the issue, so no clear majority exists. Even the other union officers are having trouble deciding here. Some believe that Guido has a point, others that it would be a very bad precedent to set if Guido were allowed to flaunt the union regulations.

You would like not to have to pursue the matter in court. However, you have discovered a recent decision concerning a related case (*Employment Division v. Smith,* U.S. Supreme Court, 1990) that is especially pertinent. In that case, the Court ruled that the First Amendment's clause guaranteeing the free exercise of religion does not apply to labor issues. In light of this decision, an attorney you consulted advised you that Guido's case has little chance of success. Moreover, the legal fees alone are more than he will be able to handle. He has no realistic chance of finding work elsewhere in Burlington and will probably have to relocate to find a job offering comparable work and pay.

All of this is what bothers you. Legally Guido seems doomed, but is it right for your union and you to force him to support causes he rejects? Ethically, this seems to violate his autonomy, religious beliefs, and personal integrity, even though he did sign on to the agreement when he needed the union and the benefits it brought him. Isn't he violating that contract and the principle of fidelity? With all this in his mind, you have to decide what to do. What options are available? Would forcing him to choose between his job and paying for causes he denies be an unfair act on your part? You are his union president, too. Would this be denying him the right to exercise his own religion? What does he, in fact, owe to the union, and how important is this obligation? Just what is your obligation to Guido and the rest of the union members in this case? Will you agree to his termination or not? Analyze the issue until it is RESOLVEDD.

32. ATV DEALER ENCOURAGES USE BY KIDS

Do You Sell a Dangerous Product to a Willing Customer?

All-terrain vehicles (ATVs) are rather squatty, big-wheeled, knobby-tired machines often seen in commercials roaring through the woods at high speeds, slashing across shallow streams, and climbing rugged hills. Such vehicles may have three or four wheels, and engines ranging from fifty to five hundred cubic centimeters in size. They look like fun, don't they? According to some private consumer groups, they look like too much fun for kids to resist. The problem, such groups say, is that although these vehicles are built for adults who know how to use them correctly, dealers have been targeting their sales for children.

In a recent national survey reported by the Ralph Nader–founded U.S. Public Interest Research Group (PIRG), almost half of the ATV dealers questioned said that ATVs designed for adults should not be used by children under the age of sixteen. However, about 75 percent of the dealers responding also agreed that children ten years of age would have very little trouble mastering the operation of an ATV. A spokesperson for the PIRG asserted that ATV dealers are continuing to mislead consumers about the dangers of ATVs even after the adoption of an agreement between the dealers and the U.S. government.

The agreement, signed in January 1988 by Honda, Suzuki, Kawasaki, Yamaha, and Polaris, all makers of ATVs, bans the sales of three-wheeled vehicles in the United States. The agreement states that only vehicles smaller than 90cc can be sold to children between the ages of twelve and sixteen. In addition, it limits the sales of larger four-wheeled ATVs to buyers sixteen years of age and older. It is the manufacturers' responsibility to notify the dealers and enforce the provisions of the agreement.

Of the dealers surveyed, 46 percent said that they would sell large four-wheel-drive ATVs knowing that children as young as ten might be using them. This practice, however, would be a violation of the agreement. Furthermore, the telephone survey revealed that 99 percent of the dealers did not inform customers that the larger, adult-sized vehicles were inappropriate for use by a ten-year-old child. In fact, fifty of the dealers admitted that they would sell machines with engines between 90 and 149cc knowing that they were intended for use by ten-year-olds. Indeed, eleven dealers said they would sell the larger, 150cc, adult vehicles for use by the young children. A spokesperson for a California PIRG stated that some dealers downplay the need for any special training in the handling of the larger machines. This also violates a part of the agreement, which calls for the manufacturers to supply free training and to add incentives for ATV purchasers and their families to take advantage of it.

The statistics compiled by the Consumer Product Safety Commission demonstrate that significant risk is associated with the use of ATVs, especially for children. In 1988, almost 40 percent of the death and injuries reported for ATVs involved children under the age of sixteen. There were 1,346 ATV deaths reported from 1982 to June 1989 and 36 for all of 1989. Of these, twenty involved four-wheel machines. Before 1985, a commission memo states, 156 people were reported killed in ATV accidents (11 four-wheel deaths), while in 1988, 112 deaths were reported for four-wheel vehicles, and 103 for three-wheel vehicles. Such statistics seem to indicate that these are vehicles to be taken seriously, even by adults, and are not the kind of toy intended for young children who may be less able to understand their dangers or know how to minimize them.

On Tuesday morning, your fifth day on the job, a man comes in to look over your selection of ATVs. You introduce yourself and tell him you'll be happy to answer any questions he has about the 125cc model that interests him. After a few questions about speed, acceleration, and how easy the ATV is to operate, he says, "I'm sold! My kid's gonna love this thing. He's been asking about one for three weeks since he saw a commercial on TV, with the guys jumpin' the hills and the river. His eleventh birthday will be a big one, alright."

"He's eleven?" you ask.

"Not until next Friday. But what the heck, I might as well buy it today, right? He'll be able to handle it. He's a strong kid."

You hesitate, a puzzled look on your face. Marty, who's been listening to your sales technique, steps over and says, "Right you are, sir! This baby's so easy to handle that a real baby could run it with no special training."

"Great! Well, wrap her up. I'll pay with my American Express."

"Ring it up," Marty says, pointing at you as he walks into the back room.

It is a $3,000 sale, for which you will receive a 5 percent commission. This is your second sale and your fifth day on a job that will provide your tuition in the fall. The money is exciting to you, and so is the sweet smell of success.

What should you do? Examine your options and the implications of each in light of your own knowledge and responsibility in the case. You must make a decision, once you have analyzed the case until it is RESOLVEDD.

33. COFFEE, TEA, OR THE SALE? ▆▆▆▆▆▆▆▆▆▆
A Clash between Japanese and
American Treatment of Women

You have had a reputation for efficiency, brilliance, and the ability to sell computers and business systems to the most reluctant corporate clients. As a result, you are the senior sales representative and vice president of Business Office Systems (BOS). You also have the reputation of being a pioneer for women's rights in the corporate world. You have fought discrimination for over twenty years on your way to the top. Now you may have to overlook some of your feminist principles while negotiating your first sale to a Japanese company.

You have done your research. You have studied the Japanese way of doing business, reading late into the night about the differences between the Japanese and American corporate cultures. You know that during negotiations, Japanese body language differs from American body language and that you must not misread the signals. Timing, etiquette, and cultural details differ. But you are set to do business in the Japanese way. The sale of a multimillion-dollar computer system to Oyakawa International Bank rides on your ability to convince the four Japanese executives at today's meeting.

You also know, to your dismay, that women in executive positions in Japanese firms are not treated like their male counterparts. This practice bothers you, especially because one of the executives you would be dealing with is a woman. While doing your research, you have read a newspaper article that outlined the way in which women in Japanese businesses are treated. According to the article, Japanese men expect that women will not put in the time and work necessary to succeed in the tough world of Japanese business. Moreover, female executives often serve as waitresses during business meetings! Yet none of this is taken as sexist, and a Japanese woman executive is quoted as saying, "It would be unthinkable to protest this treatment, especially when I'm on a career track." The fact is that only 1 percent of executives in Japan are women, although women make up 40 percent of the workforce. The double standard in Japanese business is widely accepted, including dress codes at some companies that require all women employees, from filing clerks to vice presidents, to wear the same blue suits.

As the meeting began with the four executives of Oyakawa International, you hoped that it would pass quickly, with no cultural conflicts. But it was not long before this began to look like a false hope. The Oyakawa negotiating team included two men and the woman, all of roughly the same rank. The third man, however, had higher rank than the others and considerably more experience. However, the other two men had considerably less experience than their female counterpart. About thirty minutes into the meeting, the senior officer said something in Japanese to Ms. Akiyama. She nodded, left, and returned about five minutes later with coffee and donuts for everyone present.

Despite your background reading and research, you were mildly shocked to see this in practice but tried not to let on. The negotiations proceeded smoothly for another forty minutes. You felt sure that Oyakawa Bank was going to buy the whole systems package your chosen account representative had prepared. Caroline Knight and her assistant, Delia Star, were your best reps. They had negotiated almost all of BOS's biggest contracts and had put together an exceptional package for Oyakawa. There were no other people at your firm that you would trust with such a lucrative account, even if some of your other reps were familiar with the Oyakawa account.

So what followed next at the meeting was a real shocker for you. At this point, the senior officer again addressed his associates in Japanese. They all nodded again and again, Ms. Akiyama included. They were smiling and nodding at you the whole time the senior officer spoke to them. You watched Ms. Akiyama closely, and she was smiling very enthusiastically at you, so you thought she was indicating that you were about to be awarded the contract.

Before you could begin to feel good about the deal, the senior officer of Oyakawa said to you, "We are very pleased with your proposal and would like to finalize this deal. Would you be so kind as to grant us just one request, however?"

"Of course, if I—rather, we—can!" was your immediate reply. But the request floored you.

"Wonderful. We are very pleased to be having you handle our account, but we would very much prefer if you could have your best men take over now. We appreciate the work you and your helpers have done so far, but we would feel much more comfortable with male account reps. You understand, don't you?"

This whole plan was your, Caroline, and Delia's creation. It also seemed clear that what the senior officer meant was that he did not expect to close the deal with you, a woman, or have women handle his firm's account after the deal was closed. You thought that he probably did not realize what a breach of American corporate culture had just occurred. He probably had no idea how insulting you found his request. As you were about to say something in response, the senior officer added, "And could you please have your assistants there bring us more of your excellent coffee? It has been a long day with too much talking, don't you think?"

This was it! Not only had he presumed that you would not object to his request and dismissal of you and your staff, not only had he constantly been sexist in his treatment of his female colleague, but now he expected your account reps to cater to his wishes for coffee as well. The insult might have been easier for you to take but for the problems it created for Caroline and Delia, as well as your firm. Your first instinct was to tell him off and give him a lecture on feminism in business, but you caught yourself.

"Stop and take a deep breath. This is a multimillion-dollar sale," you think. How can you handle this in such a way as to protect your own dignity, but not insult your clients? Is that possible? Must you just meekly give in for the sake of the sale? Different cultures are one thing—you were ready for some adjustments—but demeaning treatment is another. This violates every belief you have about equality for women in the workplace.

It strikes you that this sexism is not all that much different than requesting someone of the "right" race as an account rep. Beyond all this is the fact that both Caroline and Delia deserve the account and all the income from commissions it would generate for them. Then, too, you actually have no one else who's ready to handle the account. Can you tell your clients that? But why should you have to, anyway? This is America, and Caroline and Delia are the best people Oyakawa could have handling the account. Even if they wanted to step down and you agreed, there would be no one able to take over, and the account would have to be dropped. You could try to explain this but have a feeling it would do no good. The senior officer clearly prefers a male account executive.

Isn't the customer always right? Or is this a case of unfair discrimination that you cannot honor? Would you be replacing them if they were, say, black and your client objected to them for that reason? And, after all, don't you owe more than this to Caroline and Delia? What might they think of you and the firm they thought they could count on for fair treatment? But don't you also have a duty to your firm to bring in business? If replacing female account reps with male reps will do it, shouldn't you try? Although this is a remote possibility, could Caroline or Delia sue you for discriminatory treatment if you take them off the account after all their work? These are just some of the thoughts running through your head as you analyze this problem until it is RESOLVEDD. With a multimillion-dollar account on the line, can you afford to offend your prospective client?

34. OFFICE GOSSIP
Should You Act on Rumor or Respect Privacy?

It had never seemed to you that gossip among company employees presented any ethical issues. You always thought that gossip is simply unreliable, potentially hurtful, and best avoided. But now, as the manager of a sales group for industrial biocides and its small office staff, you are faced with a sticky ethical problem created by gossip among your staff.

One of your best salespeople, Lilly Kropov, a married woman, seems to be romantically involved with a married man, Keith Laski, who is a buyer for one of your largest accounts. You have just discovered that the five members of your office staff and your ten salespeople have talked about little else now for more than a month. Indeed, the stories have grown juicier and juicier, including references to sightings of the couple together overseas on business trips and a sexual encounter in Lilly's office after hours. The latter was detected by an unsuspecting janitor who happened to hear noises from the office before he turned on the lights one evening. However, you have no idea how the couple could have arranged to meet overseas on a business trip, although you do regular business with companies in Southeast Asia, as does Laski's company.

Your problem stems from the fact that three of your salespeople and all but one of the office staff are well known to be thoroughly disgusted by the affair. They have been expressing disgust to each other, talking openly about it and apparently spreading the rumors. This caused you considerable embarrassment when you learned that your boss had discovered the whole thing before you did! In a meeting with him late last week, he surprised and embarrassed you by ordering you to talk to your people, silence them, and stop these rumors now before they spread to higher echelons of the company. He made it clear that if you need to fire someone to purge the company of this cancer, he will stand behind you.

You were at first puzzled as to why your boss was so adamant about what seemed at first to be a private and personal matter unrelated to work. But the dimensions of the whole thing have become increasingly clear. Your company is proud of its record in the local community, encouraging family values, community involvement of its employees, and religious affiliations. Lilly has two children in grade school and a husband on the local school board, and she attends the same church as some of the company's top executives. She and her family are highly visible and respected members of the community.

For someone with Lilly's prominence and success to be so strongly reviled by her coworkers is a significant matter. This point became even clearer to you earlier this week when Lilly stormed into your office with some pretty strong demands. It seems that some other coworkers in the company had left some suggestive, anonymous messages and limericks in her office. She brought three of them in to you and demanded that you take steps to put an end to them at once. When you asked Lilly what prompted them, you received a hostile response to the effect that it is none of your business and none of the person's who had left her the dirty notes. Her life is her own business, and you need to respect separation of work and personal life. You have the power and influence to stop the notes, and you need to take action now!

At this point it seemed clear that you needed to have a meeting with the rest of your staff. But that merely exacerbated the problem. When you met this morning with all available, which included everyone but Lilly and two other salespeople who happened to be out of town, the intransigence of the problem emerged. More than half of those present expressed open hostility and resentment toward Lilly, insisting venomously that you should terminate her work with the company. Your explanation of why you need to end all this talk and these childish and dangerous anonymous notes was met with the retort that you should fire Lilly now before it all blows up.

You responded to those present by telling them that they have no business being so judgmental of the lives of others. They in turn said that Lilly was ruining the lives of her husband and children, destroying a beautiful family, and that this is in fact a community issue and a matter for the company to address directly. The failure to do so will only bring disrepute to you and the company, which has no obligation to continue to employ people who are immoral and untrustworthy. The implication is that when higher management finds out you have let this fester, your career will be damaged.

The other workers reacted by saying that because Lilly was carrying on with a buyer, it seemed to them that she was the one who needed to be disciplined. How can you allow her to continue in this way? Won't someone get the idea that doing well in the company depends on having an affair with a buyer? You have to admit that this raises another significant issue, namely that of company morale. Will other employees, hearing the gossip or finding out that it's true, feel they are at a disadvantage? Won't this hurt Lilly's reputation as a professional in her field? If so, should you allow her to claim that her private life is private and let it go at that? It certainly seems that her private life has gotten very public and is affecting the internal and possibly external atmosphere surrounding your company. Maybe it should be Lilly who is "corrected," not those who started the rumors.

Your subsequent meeting with Lilly is what crystallized your problem. After you told her all that you had been told and said regarding the problem, she seethed with anger, alleging slander designed to destroy her. Yet when you asked her to tell you the facts so that you could help her out, she refused, repeating with great emotion that it was a bunch of lies that she would fight to the bitter end. However, never did she specifically deny that she had been having an affair. Her vow to fight probably meant that she intended to sue you, the company, her coworkers, and perhaps others if the gossip did not stop or if you attempted to fire her. In any case, she specified that she would talk to no one about this now but her lawyer and certainly not to anyone else in the company.

As you think it all over, several important ideas keep bothering you. What if she is right and many of the stories and allegations about her are untrue, even if the overall fact of her having an affair with Laski is true? What if, on the other hand, she is having an affair with someone other than Laski? Is it right for you to fire her on allegations of immoral conduct? If what is being said is true, don't the other workers have a right to free expression of their opinions? Maybe the anonymous notes are going too far, yet aren't other expressions of disgust and disapproval simply exercising free speech? Then again, if the rumors are true, isn't it bad business to let employees carry on with customers? This can come to no good end for your company, can it? Although you do not clearly violate any laws by firing her, she certainly could sue and win a large settlement if she could prove that you are releasing her on the basis of unsubstantiated gossip. On the other hand, on what ethical grounds does the company owe her a job if in fact she has been engaging in such immoral behavior that so clearly contradicts the values, goals, and image of the company? Finally, can she be fired because her actions are harming company morale and because she is involved in a situation that can easily affect her work? What, then, should you do to see the problem RESOLVEDD?

35. Is This the Job You Have Been Waiting For?
Can You Tolerate Environmentally Unsound Practices?

Although Just Green Corporation (JGC) has made you an offer you thought you'd never refuse, you are no longer so sure. Having just graduated from college with a B.A. in general business, you were at first pleased by the prospect of a position in their largest field office overseeing day-to-day aspects of their operation. JGC specializes in timber products and has three field offices located in different timber-producing regions. You would be working in the Washington state office.

JGC was also a part of a much larger conglomerate that owned companies that produced, literally, everything from soup to nuts with everything else in between. It was the connection with the conglomerate that was causing your indecision. After your interview with JGC, you had gone home to study the various pieces of informational literature the personnel manager had given you. When looking over one prospectus, you noticed the name of the conglomerate that owned JGC. Immediately you felt a little uneasy. The name was familiar to you but not for positive reasons. You thought at first that maybe you had it wrong. However, your uneasy feelings were confirmed by a little searching on the Internet. The conglomerate was implicated in a number of lawsuits and mentioned in the newsletters of several environmental groups as a very "nongreen" company. At least five major lawsuits were going on in which environmental groups were suing one or the other of the conglomerate's subsidiaries for environmentally damaging practices. As near as you could tell, though, JGC was not one of the subsidiaries being sued.

What bothered you about such suits was your own concern for the environment. Although you do not consider yourself an environmental fanatic or activist, you do worry about many of the dire predictions scientists have made in the last few years. In particular, the destruction of the remaining old growth timber in the United States and wholesale cutting of rain forests in South America were on your mind. It seemed to you that it was just common sense to say that people could not just keep cutting down forests, even if they were replanted, without either eventually using up all the timber that remained or causing the destruction of a natural habitat for many animals and plants. You are aware of the extensive documentation that shows that old growth forests are profoundly different from replanted second- and third-growth forests, despite what many timber industry spokespeople say.

On the other hand, you are also aware that reputable scientists disagree with the dire predictions of ecological disasters. There is some conflicting opinion among experts about whether cutting the rain forests is a cause of the hole in the ozone layer, global warming if it truly is happening, or a host of other items listed by the environmental groups. The evidence is very difficult to weigh and understand given its highly technical nature, as well as the fact that the disasters being forecast are speculation, not proven facts.

Perhaps you could feel a little better about working for this conglomerate if you simply chose to believe that the doomsayers were wrong and everything would be OK. However, you can't quite convince yourself that it is safe to ignore so much scientific evidence. Maybe, you had thought, if you examined JGC carefully, it would turn out that they were a responsible "green" company just as their name suggests.

That was when you realized that you had a difficult decision to make. The literature the personnel director supplied looked very reassuring, of course. It contained many statements designed to give the reader the impression that JGC was following all the latest environmentally conscious practices used in the logging industry. Yet when you had read more of the environmentalists' literature from the Internet, it seemed that JGC was guilty of exaggerating its commitment to sound environmental precautions. In fact, one rather radical Web site implicated JGC in clear-cutting, the complete deforestation of an area that leads to erosion and destruction of the soil and all animal habitats in the clear-cut area. There was a picture of a clear-cut area that looked as if someone had firebombed the side of a mountain. The picture was not of any area logged by JGC, though. But if JGC followed the same process anywhere, it meant equal damage to that area as the one pictured.

When you had called the personnel manager at JGC and expressed your concerns, he assured you that JGC did no clear-cutting anymore, though it had in the past. He told you that JGC had eliminated the practice following the guidelines of all governmental agencies and knowledgeable environmentalists. When you pressed for names of individuals in these agencies or the specific environmentalists, he had basically dodged the question and simply kept repeating the company's claims as if he were reading out of the same literature he had given you. You were less than certain JGC was a good, green corporate citizen. However, you were far from convinced that they were as bad as many other logging companies.

Their connection to the large conglomerate still bothered you. The conglomerate was often in the news, usually as the object of protests, lawsuits, and government actions against it for some unethical or illegal activity. Not all of the activity was connected to environmental issues. Some were questionable investment practices, violations of agreements with foreign governments, unethical hiring practices, and other such activities. The environmentalist groups also listed four of its subsidiaries in the top ten offenders against the earth. Again, JGC was not one of the companies listed.

You couldn't shake the worry, however, that if JGC was owned by a conglomerate with this reputation for being unethical, nongreen and for breaking the law, it would be engaging in similar activities itself.

Try as you might, you couldn't uncover any hard evidence that JGC was guilty of any illegal actions or of causing massive environmental damage. There were a few small incidents and legal warnings that followed them in which JGC had caused minor damage to the environment. These included using a bleaching agent that was slightly stronger than allowed by law at one of the paper mills JGC owned and taking about 2 percent more old growth timber than the law allowed in the last fiscal year. These seemed almost unavoidable transgressions to you, though. After all, a company the size of JGC was bound to run afoul of some law sooner or later, especially environmental restrictions.

Now you had to decide. Can you accept the job with JGC or not? What do you owe to yourself? The money they offered was exceptionally good. You would be moving into middle management immediately upon having graduated with a B.A., which would make you the only member of your class to do so, at least as far as you could tell. But are JGC and its parent corporation responsible companies? If JGC is, it seems clear that its parent is not. Are you going to be contributing to destructive and harmful practices if you become JGC's branch manager? Do you owe anything to future generations and the earth itself? And, even if you do, is it clear that working for JGC violates such duties? Who are you harming if you merely oversee JGC's office? Could you get into position to rectify any questionable practices, or would you get dragged into becoming a participant? What kind of pressure might come from the conglomerate?

Although these are all important questions, time is running out on JGC's offer. The personnel director had said he needed your answer in two days. Can your concerns be RESOLVEDD before then?

36. AN ETHICAL SURVEY
Should You Follow the Law Even If It Harms Someone?

Citizen's Gas Company hired you and Felicia Alden, independent surveyors located in a nearby county, to map the property line between two farms. The reason for the survey, they said, was because they had to be sure who owned the land they needed to lay a new pipeline. The problem was that Mr. Mander, who owned one of the farms, had refused to give permission to lay the line on his property. Mrs. Kildare, a widow, said they could lay the line anywhere on her property, which adjoined Mr. Mander's.

This was good news for the gas company, as only a small slice of land was geologically suitable for the pipeline. It seemed that the slice of land ran almost right along the boundary between the two farms. It would cost the company a great deal of money to have to lay the pipe elsewhere, because of the fact that most of the county was situated on solid bedrock that began only a few feet under the fertile topsoil. Except for this small strip of land, under which was almost pure clay, there was no inexpensive place to put the pipe. Mr. Mander warned them that they'd better be sure where his property ended and Kildare's began, or else. Felicia and you had been hired to do just that.

Following your obtaining the appropriate maps and legal descriptions, the two of you headed out to the farms. As expected, when talking to Mr. Mander, he was very unpleasant, if not downright threatening. Neither of you cared a bit for him.

Mrs. Kildare, however, was as sweet as she could be, offered you lunch, and said to take as much time as you wanted on her property, then stop by for coffee and cake. During your visit to her house, you noticed that she seemed to be struggling to make ends meet, the furniture was old and worn, as were the rugs and her clothes. She even remarked that if it weren't for her land, she'd be almost completely broke.

You both went to work plotting the boundary lines between the Mander and Kildare farms. After about an hour you began to recheck all your findings against the maps and legal descriptions. There was a major problem. The legal descriptions and maps didn't match the fence line or the boundaries that Mrs. Kildare said marked her property. In fact, her property line was about twenty feet onto Mr. Mander's farm. An old fence stood there, but no matter how you rechecked all the figures, it was clear that Mr. Mander owned all the land the gas company was interested in. Moreover, Mrs. Kildare was going to lose a sizable chunk of real estate once the gas company filed the survey.

Felicia and you skipped the return visit with Mrs. Kildare and a week later turned in your report to the gas company. You received your check but went away feeling bad for Mrs. Kildare. But what could you do—the legal boundaries were set. You were feeling guilty for not telling her but didn't have the heart to do it.

Six months later you had completed a job near Mrs. Kildare's farm and decided to stop in to express your concern over what the survey had shown. When she saw you at the door, Mrs. Kildare welcomed you as an old friend. Before you could say anything, she told you that the gas company had purchased the rights to lay the pipeline on her property and for a very generous sum. She said the money was making a big difference to her.

Upon making a visit to the boundary area, you noticed that Citizen's Gas had installed the gas line as originally planned, for warning signs were posted indicating the presence of an underground pipeline. Then you noticed that the old fence on Mr. Mander's property was exactly where it had been six months earlier. The markers ran right along the Kildare side of the fence, but you know they are well inside the Mander property. Citizen's Gas had apparently ignored your survey report and gone ahead with its original plans as if Mrs. Kildare owned the property. Apparently, it had not filed the survey with the county. Citizen's Gas was evidently disregarding both the truth and the law.

Knowing that you both have some professional responsibility as certified public surveyors, you and Alden wrote a letter to Citizen's Gas advising it of the apparent problem. You received no acknowledgment of your letter and saw no evidence that it had any effect. When Felicia called the gas company, she was put on hold for twenty minutes before being cut off. It seemed you were being completely ignored. Now what? What should you do?

On the one hand, you have accurate and reliable knowledge of an ongoing violation of the law. You both have a professional ethical obligation not to be parties to fraud. To fail to pursue the problem might be a violation of professional ethics or the law.

On the other hand, to take further action would harm all the wrong people. It would ultimately deprive poor Mrs. Kildare of much needed cash, give extra, unneeded support to the unpleasant Mr. Mander, and likely cost Citizen's Gas a pretty penny. Finally, it would ensure that you would not receive any further business from Citizen's and might well damage your reputations.

Is there any way out of this difficult situation? Analyze the case until you have RESOLVEDD the important issues, all things considered.

37. TO TELL OR NOT TO TELL? ▬▬▬▬▬▬
Abortion Counseling and the New "Gag" Rule

The Supreme Court has upheld a law requiring federally funded family planning clinics that counsel women on birth control to abstain from providing any information on abortion options. In the state where you live, additional strict guidelines have been passed by the legislature dictating what a clinic may do when clients request information about abortion. The guidelines, as they now stand, instruct counselors to say, "I'm sorry, I cannot provide any information of that sort. Abortion is not considered an acceptable form of birth control."

You are a counselor at a private clinic that specializes in family planning but also provides full health care. The clinic receives federal grant money and treats many people whose health care is paid by federal dollars. The new legislation has restricted your options as a counselor and thus reduced your professional effectiveness. You resent the restriction on your professional judgment. However, you also respect the law and do not believe that you ought to violate it. You certainly do not want any of your actions to jeopardize the clinic's license.

Last week, however, the director of the clinic, an internist with thirty-five years of experience in family practice, called a meeting of the staff. He explained that the first responsibility of all clinic employees is the well-being of the patients. He cited the codes of ethics of several health care professions to support his belief.

"Personally," he said, "I think the new laws violate our freedom of speech and destroy the doctor-patient relationship." He went on to explain that what a doctor told a patient was private and that the government had no business limiting the doctor's options for treatment. Such limitations endanger patients and, in effect, force the whole medical profession to commit malpractice. He concluded by advising the counselors to ignore the new legal restrictions and to counsel patients as they always had.

Immediately after the meeting, you discussed some of the issues with other members of the staff. Some of the counselors argued that there is a constitutional right to an abortion, as *Roe v. Wade* established, and any legislation violating that right should be ignored. One member of the staff quoted Dr. Martin Luther King's statement that people have no duty to obey unjust laws. He then pointed out that depriving women of one of their legal rights by arbitrary legislation was certainly unjust. He urged everyone to perform an act of civil disobedience and to continue giving information about abortion to anyone who requested it.

Some other staff members, like yourself, said that violating the law, even for the best interests of the patient, should not be done lightly. One man insisted that the fetus should also be considered a patient, whose interests we must respect as well. Another staff member expressed fear that the clinic would lose its government funding, thus harming patients on welfare and all who could not otherwise pay for the clinic's services.

The discussion lasted for over an hour. When you left, you were aware that the director thought that he could get private funding to cover the loss of government support. But you also realized that violation of the new restrictions would be against the law. The meeting caused you to feel the conflict in a personal way. You knew that you would soon need to take sides on the matter and that to do this you would need to make up your own mind on what is best under the circumstances. Specifically, the question is what you should do in the case.

To decide what your role should be in the case, you must determine whether you have a stronger duty to the mission of the clinic or to the law. Is your duty to the law more important than the patients' right to information and informed consent and the health professionals' right to advise openly and honestly according to conscience and to practice in the patient's best interest? What should you as a responsible citizen and employee do in such a case? You will need to consider these questions and the broad picture to have this case RESOLVEDD.

38. BUYING STOCK AND SELLING ONE'S SOUL
Should You Avoid a Potential Conflict of Interest?

As a newly hired finance officer for an established brokerage firm with an excellent reputation for both success and honesty, you had, for your first six months with the firm, been riding a wave of enthusiasm. And your new assignment in the company has already presented you with an exciting opportunity, even if it is a chance to profit from the misfortunes of others. But now you are realizing that the choice involves ethical as well as financial risk, and you must weigh the values at stake and the possible consequences of your options.

Your supervisor is the well-known and highly successful senior account executive, Carol Sakawi. Carol had assigned you to a number of new accounts during your first four months at the firm, and you had picked up a clear sense of the attitude of senior management toward the credit status of various corporate clients. The company seemed to take, in most cases, a moderate approach to credit risk, reducing the credit of clients only when such reductions were clearly demonstrated. Furthermore, you found that Carol, like other senior account executives in this particular firm, usually takes the recommendations of her subordinates regarding changes in the credit status of clients. So you were finding the firm to be a congenial environment in which to work and also, in one particular case, financially promising.

You were assigned to the important account of the Lone Star Bank Holding Corporation just two weeks ago. Carol had told you of rumors that Lone Star was in financial straits, and she assigned you to investigate them immediately together with

Mr. Harvey Washington, another young finance analyst assigned temporarily from another department. You and Harvey decided together that he would talk directly with the Lone Star executives and you would investigate the supposed sources of the rumors. By the end of the first week on this assignment, a complex of events had taken place that had your head spinning.

By the end of the second day, the rumors had led you nowhere except to documentation of the fact that several top executives of Lone Star had, during the past month, sold off large blocks of their stock in the company! Given the actual information about the company in the hands of the public, there was no good explanation of why this had happened. Indeed, one might suspect insider trading on the part of these executives! So you began to wonder whether something big and bad was about to happen.

Harvey, however, found absolutely nothing of significance: not even a suggestive clue. From his perspective, everything seemed to be normal and financially sound. It was Tuesday evening, shortly after you had both agreed on further avenues to explore tomorrow, when the bombshells hit. And both came to you, of all places, on the evening news! First a news story aired that the local newspaper had reported earlier in the day that Lone Star was going to declare tomorrow a $12.1 million loss for the quarter. Then there was news that the securities commissioner of your state had suspended trading of Lone Star stock. You were stunned and called Harvey at once.

The significance of all this was that you had clearly failed to provide your brokerage with any advance warning of the impending crisis. This might reflect poorly on Carol and the two of you. It would be especially bad if Lone Star had made any major leveraged stock or bond purchases that day. You could hardly wait to find out.

Once on line and into the brokerage's computer, it was clear what had happened. Lone Star had actually leveraged the purchase of a huge block of its own stock before noon that day. So the Lone Star management was apparently acting to prop up the price of company shares by borrowing money from your brokerage! By hiding the real information from you and Harvey, Lone Star had smoothly and successfully used brokerage money to take a major first step in defending itself against collapse. You and Harvey, a couple of rookies, had been played the fools! What next?

Wednesday was a whirlwind of discoveries, consultations, and decisions. Carol stayed calm and tolerant under the circumstances, Harvey seemed nervous, and the Lone Star executives understandably reticent. One tidbit of information that you discovered late in the day was particularly interesting. Lone Star was scheduled to auction off, the next day, a block of stock with a book value of $7 per share. You knew it would sell for far less than that. And you also thought that Lone Star would, before long, come out of the financial crisis once it spun off two miserable small banks it had acquired last year from a hostile takeover in West Virginia. You knew the auction was possibly a rare, even if risky opportunity. And the securities commissioner had already decided to allow this particular auction to take place. So you prepared to spend $4,000 on as much stock as you could get.

On Thursday, at noon, you found out that you were the owner of twenty thousand shares of Lone Star stock! You had succeeded in picking it up for 20 cents per share by some careful bidding on-line during a midmorning break. That stock could make you rich some day, or it could possibly become worthless. But the risk was, in your view, surely worthwhile.

It was in the middle of the next week that Carol called you in for another talk. This time she seemed to have a different tone than before. And as she told you of her knowledge of your purchase of Lone Star stock, it dawned on you that there were implications of which you had not been aware. Carol raised the daunting question of a possible conflict of interest. She pointed out that you are now a stockholder in the troubled company to which your brokerage routinely lends money through stock margins and other types of loans. You are trying to profit from speculation on a future reversal of the company's misfortune.

You explained in your defense that the stock auction was public in every sense and advertised in newspapers all over town. The stories of the company's problems were public knowledge, and you had not used any privileged information.

When Carol asked whether you thought you could continue to work on the account, you said, "Of course." Your job is to recommend to your brokerage the best policy for granting stock margins and other forms of loans to the bank holding company. Such matters are irrelevant to decisions about personal stock holdings in Lone Star. Naturally you know that under certain possible future circumstances, your conduct could become highly suspect. If, for example, the holding company's stock and credit rating drops further, as it well may, and you continue to recommend that its credit at your brokerage remain the same, it may appear as though you are trying to prop up the holding company in bad times to facilitate its recovery. If your superiors then discover that Carol knew what you did about the case and allowed you to continue, you and Carol may well both lose your jobs.

Carol, in her characteristic and kind way, has asked you to advise her on the realities, the risks, and the best course of action for you and for her given the circumstances. Of course, you know that the decision is, in the end, hers. But you also feel convinced that she really does want your honest and considered opinion on what to do. So you promise to think it over carefully and give her a full report next Monday.

The problem you face is how seriously to take the potential conflict of interest. It is very clearly at this point only potentially a conflict of interest. But is that acceptable to you, and should it be acceptable to other managers? Many options are available to you at this point, and you will need to assess carefully the ethical and practical considerations to see the case RESOLVEDD.

39. FIDELITY TO THE UNION OR ITS MEMBERS?
Negotiating, Selling Out, or Serving the Union's Interests

As the junior contract negotiator for the garment workers' union in talks with a major designer of popular clothing, you are troubled by the viewpoint shared by other members of the team. They want to agree to a proposal which you think is a sellout and that would benefit the union but not three hundred workers of a certain factory who are just now becoming unemployed. The proposed deal would provide each worker with $3,000 severance pay and the union with a total of $10 million over the next three years. If that sounds pretty good on the surface and in public, the devil is in the details. You know that in reality the workers will not get what would have been expected, the union will get more, and the designer will save in the neighborhood of $10 million. Can you let this go through and still live with yourself?

The deal has been formulated largely by the negotiators for the designer in an attempt to reduce their liability for millions of dollars in "liquidated damages." These are payments allowed by an act of Congress in the 1950s that gives special freedom to the once large and now small unions of the garment industry. This law specifically prohibits all unions in all industries except the garment industry from requiring employers to do business with unionized companies. However, the garment unions can negotiate with a designer to require it to buy garments only from unionized factories. If the designer violates the agreement, the union can require the designer to pay the union a negotiated fee for each garment purchased from a nonunion manufacturer. Congress created this exemption to give some strength to the garment unions. Because designers subcontract the manufacturing of most of their garments to small, independent companies that are geographically dispersed, unions must fight one location at a time to become established. Unless the unions are free to negotiate limits to the buying practices of the designers, those designers seeking only nonunion manufacturers would soon succeed in completely eliminating unions from the manufacturing industry.

Although the liquidated damages per garment are set by each contract, the designer never pays the agreed amount per garment without challenging the allegations of the union before an arbitrator. And binding arbitration does not always bring the union the amount it alleges to be owed. In fact, unions typically receive 40 to 70 percent of their claims. Moreover, the percentage has been declining in recent years, and so, too, have the dollar figures of total liquidated damages. The present negotiations include discussions over an arbitration claim for liquidated damages alleged to amount to $40 million. Although the claim has been filed, the arbitrator has agreed to hold off the ruling until after the negotiations for the next contract are completed. So the present negotiations include the per-garment dollar figure for future liquidated damages and the figure for past liquidated damages as well as other matters.

Severance pay is a major negotiating issue. In some such cases, designers have paid as much as five times the present offer per worker. However, in other cases, unemployed workers have received no severance pay at all. And if the present amount seems small, the union could always supplement it by giving each worker some money from the liquidated damages. In reality, however, this has rarely happened, and whether it does is not a matter for a negotiating team to decide.

The proposed agreement will provide the total $10 million to the union over three years in exchange for discontinuing the pending arbitration case. In addition, the proposed settlement commits the union to receiving no more than $2 million per year for liquidated damages in the next three years of the contract. So the proposed agreement brings the union a total of $16 million in the next three years. This $5.33 million per year would constitute approximately 20 percent of the union's budget for each of those years.

The proposal is a sellout in your view because it grants low severance pay in exchange for a set, definite amount of liquidated damages. That is, the workers receive little and the union receives a lot from the proposal. What has happened is that the union has worked harder to obtain funds for its coffers and has bargained away severance pay for the workers.

You expect that some workers will figure out the nature of the deal that was struck and perhaps decide to sue the union. Your teammates disagree, pointing out that unions have always kept liquidated damages for their own use and that there is no evidence that the severance pay was ever going to be higher than it ended up. In fact, however, you know that the union had started negotiations by asking for over $23,000 of severance pay per worker and that the offer would give the union almost exactly what it had asked for in liquidated damages. Of course, it had taken more than a month to arrive at the current proposed settlement, after lengthy discussion of offers and demands of all kinds. This process had revealed clearly to you the willingness of your teammates to accept less for the workers in exchange for more for the union. And it is this point that bothers you the most. Because the union undoubtedly exists to benefit its constituent members, one would think that the team members have a primary commitment to the workers. In fact, however, the team members are evaluated by the union management, which you know wants the liquidated damages for its budget. So it is no mystery why your teammates are primarily concerned to bring home the bacon for the union. The question is what, if anything, you should do about it.

The month of negotiations had resulted in extensive familiarity among the other five members of your negotiating team. Ranging in age from forty to sixty, the others knew of your commitment to the newly unemployed workers and your reluctance to recommend the proposal to the union. In one discussion the senior negotiator commented, "Look, there's no point in giving prize money to the losing horse. These [three hundred soon to be unemployed] workers are leaving the union, anyway. For us to get them more money will bring no benefit to the union members who remain. And we work for them, not the discontinued workers."

The proposal is about to be passed along to the union whether you like it or not, and you now have a decision to make. You can either drop your disagreement and line up with the rest of the team, or you can file a minority report. To do the latter would be unusual and almost certainly lead to the end of your job with the union. This would not be a promising step for the career of a young labor negotiator in one's first job and second year of work. You know, however, that keeping quiet may also well lead to trouble. You read in the newspaper just last year about a similar case in which the newly unemployed workers of a firm in New York sued their union for selling them out after making a similar deal with the designer Liz Claiborne. If you were subpoenaed in a similar suit, you would have to tell the truth anyway, as would others on the team. Perhaps it is because the others are older, inclined to do business as usual, and had not heard or read about the case that they showed so little interest in your viewpoint. In any case, your knowledge could, perhaps, give you grounds to approach the union management with a complaint about the proposal.

If you do lose your job, you could always turn in a report to the Department of Labor. This might spark an investigation and renegotiations. But doing so might have an impact on your future employment opportunities. If you do nothing, thus aiding and abetting such lack of union fidelity to its members, you can be sure that the values behind such practices will continue to dominate the thinking of union negotiators. Such results will no doubt continue to be interpreted by union members as one more failure of the union movement, thus leading to its further decline. In the end, strong unions can strengthen the position of the American worker and thus the economy, as Congress knows well. But unions committed to fattening their own budgets at the expense of their workers will surely continue to feed their own decline.

Analyze the case, make your personal choice, and justify it until it is RESOLVEDD.

40. RESPONSIBLE FOR MY OWN NEGLIGENCE
Contractual Obligations, Trade Secrets, and a New Job

You have been the director of personnel with Satyricon Industries for the past six months. Satyricon is a new and rapidly growing banking consultant firm that specializes in clarifying, coordinating, consolidating, and refinancing the accounts of various types of firms. The job had gone well so far, but you now wondered whether you were about to violate the terms of your previous employment contract. And you wonder whether your career is dead in the water as a result of your own stupidity and the scheming of experienced managers preying on the talent of a young, innocent, and inexperienced professional.

You worked previously for four years at Fellini & Sons Consulting, a competitor of Satyricon, but older and larger. You had been hired while in college as a personnel trainee and given tuition to complete your M.A. in personnel management, which you finished with the highest honors and at the very top of your class. You were proud that your professors recognized your talent and that they expressed confidence that you had a bright future in the best of corporations.

Your opportunities at Fellini were exemplary. The executive vice president of the company had told you that Fellini was a company with only one major problem: its approach to personnel management was old-fashioned and in fact crippling, holding back creativity and progress in a number of ways. You had the distinct feeling that she in fact viewed you as the new blood that could revive an old, major, successful corporation that had slowed in growth.

At Fellini, in less than two full years, you had worked your way up to assistant director of personnel. In that position, using the skills acquired in graduate school, you devised and implemented a number of innovative personnel management approaches. These had helped Fellini hire the right kinds of people necessary for their job openings. In addition, you developed a format for employee profiles that had been used to match Fellini's personnel with their customers. As a result, Fellini was able to assign the right people at the right time to suit their customers' needs.

Your successes had taken tremendous work and struggle against opposing forces. Your boss, Irma Trapp, the director of personnel, who was nearing retirement age, was your main opposition. But you were able to overcome it by going to other managers above her, such as the executive vice president, for support. You knew she hated you but thought that you might some day replace her.

When Joe Cartwright of Satyricon contacted you to become director of personnel, you had immediately notified Irma Trapp of the offer. She explained that Fellini valued your work highly, but that further promotion would not be coming soon. She planned to continue to work for at least another decade and suggested that you negotiate for the best deal from Satyricon and then inform her to give her a chance to match the offer.

As you expected, Fellini could not guarantee you promotion to the same position or income level that Satyricon offered. After lengthy discussions with Ms. Trapp and another higher manager, you decided not to let this opportunity pass. Satyricon's significant potential for growth and your role in it would offer you an extraordinarily bright future. In addition, the job would give you a chance to formulate important policies and use your talents to their utmost.

During your last two weeks at Fellini, your associates had been encouraging and wished you well. They even held a small party for you at your final personnel meeting. The next day, Ms. Trapp invited you into her office for what she called a "farewell interview." She praised your work and expressed confidence in your future at Satyricon, pointing out that she took pride in your growth and would be watching your career advance in the future with a certain personal satisfaction. She also wanted to refresh your memory about the terms of your contract at Fellini and the "separation clause." This statement included the provision that no employee leaving Fellini could use trade secrets if later employed by a competitor. You had signed an agreement to this effect years ago and fully intended to honor your agreement. You reassured her of your intent.

It was exactly the "separation clause" that bothered you now, six months later. You had reached a point at Satyricon at which you needed to make some major changes in policy. Until now, you had merely been cleaning up loose ends and sloppy procedures, as well as trying to build a stronger team spirit in Satyricon's workforce. This had contributed to a small but noticeable increase in their efficiency and profits. But now the time had come for some basic restructuring.

Your first reaction was to implement the appropriate strategies that had worked so well at Fellini. It was then that you were reminded of Ms. Trapp's parting lecture at Fellini. The strategies you developed at Fellini resulted from its support of your education and from contributions by your colleagues with whom you consulted and collaborated at Fellini. Furthermore, as far as you knew, among firms in this industry, only Fellini was using the kinds of personnel techniques you had developed there.

The problem became acute when you consulted a lawyer to determine whether your contract with Fellini implied that you could not use the same management techniques and policies you developed at Fellini. Much to the surprise of your lawyer and you, the contract you had signed indicated specifically that! It referred to "development of innovative management strategies, techniques, and styles" that you might develop at Fellini as "trade secrets." You were being held hostage by your own freely given word!

Your lawyer advised you that this was peculiar because "trade secrets" usually refers to production processes, product composition and manufacturing, technical formulations, and other proprietary and privy information that was created by a company and is crucial to its competitive advantage. He had never heard of trade secrets including management techniques. They are in general not secret or proprietary or confidential. And it is widely believed that the manner in which management techniques are instituted is as responsible for management success as the actual techniques themselves. Furthermore, management techniques are public knowledge, published widely and regularly in professional and academic management periodicals. How could Fellini require you to restrict the use of such techniques and thus, in effect, claim ownership of them?

As you and your lawyer reflected further on Fellini's point of view, it became clear that there is indeed some justification for it. Fellini hired you with the intent that you would use your creativity to create for them a unique personnel management strategy. You did so with the help of some of their own managers. The contract you signed was tantamount to an admission by you that Fellini is the owner of what you created. Such a contract, although unusual in business management, is not uncommon in other aspects of business. Thus, corporations routinely hire educators to create personnel training programs that are subsequently owned by the corporation and to which the creator has no rights. The contract you signed indicates that you agreed to treat your new developments in such a manner, as did your confirmation to your boss at the farewell interview. Does it really matter whether these techniques are called trade secrets? You did sign a document saying you would not use such techniques elsewhere, regardless of what they're called.

Of course, your lawyer pointed out, you could sue Fellini on the grounds that their contract was unfair, unusual, abusive, and overly restrictive of your career. If, on the other hand, you were to continue on as if you never signed the contract, you would risk Fellini discovering what you had done and then filing suit. Either way, such a court battle would promise to be long and drawn out, with no likely predictable conclusion. If you lost, you would incur substantial costs.

What should you do in this harrowing situation? There are many options, each with advantages and disadvantages but also ethical values at stake. Your own reputation hangs in the balance for each of your main options. You will need to weigh them carefully as well as the demands of the relevant ethical principles to get this situation RESOLVEDD, behind you, and your life and work moving ahead.

41. PROFIT OR LOSS OF THE ENVIRONMENT?
Installing Pollution Controls That Are Not Legally Required

Your father and you had been discussing his latest idea for the family business, a small metal plating company. He had just finished reading a series of articles on the environmental problems caused by various processes used in the plating industry. Because of the caustic and toxic chemicals used in these processes, the rivers and lakes near many plating plants are dying. Those that are still viable are in serious danger of becoming polluted past the point of easy recovery. Your father, the founder and president of the company, was troubled by these articles.

Your father wanted you to set up a study of the feasibility of installing a series of purification and pollution control devices that would treat the liquid wastes leaving your plant. He gave you a number of articles that describe such devices but that did not include details about their related costs. He told you to ask Claudia Bertrand and Juan Higueras, two plant engineers, to help prepare the reports. Finally, Paulette Kaye, your accountant, was to calculate the costs involved.

The task consumed most of your time for the next month. You and Juan visited a number of facilities using similar devices but that were not in the plating industry. You obtained pollution figures from them, both before and after installation. Claudia studied the details of the devices and ways to apply them to the plating processes. It became clear that such procedures would be effective in reducing your output of pollutants.

One of Claudia's assistants, however, raised an interesting question: Why were you thinking about new pollution control equipment when the wastewater you produce is well under the legal EPA requirements? Claudia had checked the figures and pointed out that you are meeting EPA guidelines for all of the pollutants your plant discharges. The worst case was one in which your plant discharges acid at the rate of 8 parts per million (ppm), whereas the EPA standard is 10 ppm. The other toxic wastes were even further below the EPA standards.

When you raised this question with your father, he handed you a number of reports and articles that cast doubt on the EPA standards. For acid, one report recommended no more than 4 ppm, saying that anything more is a significant hazard for fish and wildlife. Your father explained that he would like the entire plant to conform to the other levels recommended in the articles.

You took the articles to Claudia and Juan, recommending their standards. You also told Paulette to calculate the costs of reducing pollutants to the levels suggested in the articles.

After four weeks, your report was complete. The various purification devices seemed more efficient than even your father expected. All of the toxic wastes produced by your plant could be cut down to the levels recommended in the articles.

The problem, of course, was the cost. Almost 40 percent of your profit margin would be eaten up by the costs of installation in the first year. After that, the costs of running and maintaining the equipment would significantly increase your production costs. To cover them, price increases or a smaller profit margin would be inevitable.

In an industry as competitive as plating, it could be disastrous to raise prices as much as you would need. No other plating companies are using the new purification devices. Most are meeting EPA standards, just as your company is. So far as you know, however, not one is even close to the recommended levels outlined in the articles. So you would be competing with companies not hampered by the costs of purification devices.

When your father read the full report, he was pleased that the devices would greatly reduce your toxic wastes. He was troubled by prospects of reduced profits but said he would be more troubled by continuing to pollute at the current levels. He suggested that the company would receive some good public relations from making such an environmentally sound decision. And he thought that the company could exploit that to its advantage.

As he looked over the figures Paulette prepared, he commented that he was sure you could remain viable and make about a 10 percent profit in prosperous years. During a recession, though, he admitted that you would have to hang on and swallow some losses once the purification devices were installed. All in all, he preferred to go ahead and install the devices. But he was willing to listen to any counterarguments you had. If you could convince him to leave well enough alone, he assured you that he would back you 100 percent. "After all, everything is legal as it is, so maybe you can convince me I'm being too demanding."

The decision is complicated. What is the price of a clear conscience? Do you have obligations that go beyond merely obeying the law? Should you do what will be most profitable for the company and its workers or not? Clearly many questions have to be RESOLVEDD.

42. No Cloaks and Daggers, Just Computers ▨
Personal Values, the Law, and Computer Spying

You have heard of computer "snoops" who tap into various data banks to obtain helpful information. You are aware that much of this snooping does not violate any laws, despite its ethically dubious nature. You know that there is even an organization, with a code of ethics, called the Society of Computer Intelligence, formed by a concerned group of computer "spies." You also have heard rumors that, in the corporate world, French and Japanese firms are masters at obtaining information this way.

You have been working for over a year as a data systems specialist at Griggs Toy Company, which has about a hundred full-time employees. The company creates new toys and games, preferring to sell its ideas to larger companies such as Mattel, though it markets some of its own creations.

Until now, you never dreamed of becoming a computer spy. It was last Monday morning that the CEO of the firm, Darren Griggs, approached you with the idea of computer spying. He explained that the time had come to delve into various data banks containing information on rival toy companies. He explained that competition is getting very stiff and that recently, foreign firms have been competing directly with American firms all over the world. Any edge would help in the competitive toy business.

Griggs pointed out that Japanese companies have been gathering computer intelligence for years and consider this a normal business practice. Because they think nothing special of it, he explained, neither should we. It is time to turn your expertise toward the gathering of information. Darren points out that the company subscribes to a large computer network database that compiles information of all sorts on toy companies and that he thought the firm could benefit from your searching the database for various bits of information about your competition's financial status.

You hesitated at first, and Griggs reacted at once by stating that you would not be doing anything illegal. "We don't want you to illegally penetrate confidential information networks or bug corporate board rooms. We just want you to tap into the network for information freely given it by its subscribers. It's all legal."

You are still a little hesitant given that your parents, devout Christians, raised you to be honest and to do unto others as you would have them do unto you, and this request seemed a bit underhanded. But Darren has convinced you it's all legal and you would be compiling only freely given data.

During one of your information-gathering sessions, your computer blinks, the screen goes black, and then comes back on. As you check to be sure you haven't lost the information you were scanning, you notice a new list of numbers next to the names of companies on the screen. You realize that these are code numbers, exactly like the one you use to access the network. You also remember that Darren told you to be careful not to disclose your code. The code allows you to access your own data bank with the network, which contains confidential information the network will not release to any other subscribers.

At that moment Darren stops by and looks over your shoulder, immediately seeing what is on the screen. "Whoa, how'd you get those numbers?" he says. You explain what happened and Darren grins and tells you to access those confidential files of the rival companies, as there is all sorts of information there that could really give you an edge in planning your new corporate budget. "This is some lucky break. We did nothing illegal and fate hands us just what we need," Darren exclaims gleefully.

"What do you mean?" you ask. "How can that give us an edge?"

"Look, our confidential file contains our budget figures, including research and development. If we know how much our competitors are spending on R and D, we can raise or lower our own budget, increase our R and D efforts, and maybe hit the market first with some new products. Who knows what else we'd learn that would give us a leg up on them?"

You don't know what to say. These files are confidential, the network would never release such information, and you'd never want your rivals to have access to your confidential file. Yet, isn't business a matter of outcompeting the other companies? Besides, you got the numbers by accident. In the same position, your competition would check your files. And you have no legal obligation to keep their files private. Because this practice doesn't violate the law, many businesspeople would consider it justifiable. You've been handed a lucky break that gives you an advantage over the competition. It's no different than finding a confidential memo on the street.

You know this is true but still feel somehow compromised and dirty. What would your father and mother think? On the other hand, many traditional Christian values are clearly inconsistent with modern corporate culture. How would it affect you to turn down this order? Should you even worry about such questions? Or should you just follow the order, accept the practice as legal, and go ahead? These issues are not easily RESOLVEDD. But you must decide now and live with the outcome.

43. A CHALLENGE TO ANTINEPOTISM POLICIES ABROAD
When in Rome Do You Do as the Romans Do?

You have been working for almost a year now as the manager in charge of a small but growing office of a multinational company in a South American country. The office has been in existence in this country for almost three years, and you are the second manager in its history. You were advised by your mentor in the corporation back home to take the position if offered because it has enormous potential for growth and could well become the central success of your career, eventually sending you right to the top of the company.

Your best salesman, Miguel Fontina, comes from a large, established, wealthy, and influential local family and was educated in the nation's leading university. Indeed, there is no doubt that some of his success in sales is due to his personal contacts with other businesspeople all over the country. With nearly half of the business you do in the country being with firms outside the local metropolitan area in which you are located, Miguel's connections are important.

The problem you are having with Miguel is based on a conflict between the stated antinepotism policies of the company and the customs and values of the indigenous population. The corporation permits the hiring of relatives of employees but requires that no relatives be allowed to work as subordinates for their relatives. It also requires no special business preferences such as lower loan rates, lower prices, or deferred payment plans be given to customers related to corporate employees. That is, the official minimums approved by the central management of the company abroad are not to be violated for any reason, including family connections.

The country you are located in, however, is famous for its family networks, cronyism, and the peddling of influence. It is a society in which the people one knows are as important in business success as what one does or accomplishes. Before leaving for your assignment here, you were warned of the complications and dangers this practice can cause and given company policies, as well as several books to read on the subject. And you are fully aware that Miguel was hired as much for his family connections as for his promise as a salesman. And now the conflict is in your office, here on your desk, and on your mind!

It came to your attention early yesterday morning when you were reviewing a large new sales bill to a company with offices that are local and in other cities in the country. Two things were clear on paper, and a third was brought forth by Miguel in person. First was the name of the customer: the Fontina Canning Company. You wondered immediately whether this was Miguel's family. Second were the price and terms of payment for your product. They were both a little below the company's stated minimum and also below the standards of your competitors. They were, moreover, low enough to virtually eliminate any profit that you might make from the sale.

It was only an hour later that Miguel came bouncing in cheerfully to your office to discuss the order. He explained that this order was a major coup for the company, as it would establish a new account with a major producer, which would replace the account that Fontina Canning had with one of your prime competitors. It would open the door to considerable new business in the future and was well worth the initial sacrificial terms that made it what is often called in business a "loss leader."

When you asked Miguel whether the Fontina Canning Company was run by his relatives, he answered that his cousins now controlled the firm, his uncle having retired just last year. When you reminded him of the corporation's antinepotism policies, he looked at you as if you were crazy. "I signed this contract for the benefit of this company, not the benefit of my cousins" was his reply.

Then you asked him whether he was receiving a kickback for the deal. He became insulted and cited company policy that kickbacks are forbidden. He next gave you a lengthy lecture on the need to be flexible in business and how the corporation needed to have an image of flexibility if it was to succeed here in South America. He explained that as a local citizen, he had a duty to help you understand the particular cultural climate of the area and that you both have a duty to promote long-term business success, not just high quarterly profits.

You said that you would think it over but that you were less than delighted with the arrangements. You explained that some rules are essential for a successful business and that choosing to violate company policy is a major decision that he should not have made on his own. You knew that you had some serious thinking to do on the matter.

Review of your notes, company policy, and your understanding of your job, its challenge, and your future clarified a number of important points for you. First, the company clearly expected you to make the decision on your own. Your boss back home had briefed you on the issues, given you all the relevant background information you needed to make the decision, and had made it clear that in South America, you would be the boss. It would clearly count against you to call him up and ask for consultation on this question. To do so would be to admit that you could not handle such a touchy situation, showing timidity and a lack of strong business leadership. Managers are not expected to go whining to their superiors every time there is a difficult decision to make. One should seek advice from above only if a decision exceeds one's authority. You had heard your boss lecture other subordinates on these points a number of times in the past.

Second, to violate company policy in such a case would be dangerous for many reasons. It would set a precedent locally and establish a reputation that would no doubt spread, thus bringing in other customers expecting similar treatment. If in the long run your many contracts lost too much money for the corporation, the reduced profits might all be left at your door. To let this go uncorrected could certainly earn you a reputation for being spineless.

On the other hand, major risks sometimes lead to great business success. Flexibility is clearly essential for a multinational company. Is Miguel right that this is a case for which the risks are well worth the likely future successes? Don't you owe it to the company to build future business?

Then, too, this was not an illegal practice but merely one that compromised internal company policy. Wouldn't the possible increase in business in the future justify this small compromise of internal policy? Aren't policies subject to the discretion of the manager in charge of the operation, so long as they do not subject the company to legal action? Besides, when in Rome, or South America, shouldn't an American company do as the Romans and South Americans do? Foremost in your mind now is whether following corporate policy is really acting faithfully to the company. Is it in any way unethical to realize the limitations of company policy to advance the business? In the end, what is most important in deciding your best course of action and getting the case RESOLVEDD?

44. FAIR PRICING PRACTICES? ▪▪▪▪▪▪▪▪▪▪▪▪▪▪▪▪▪
Should You Take Advantage of Circumstances?

"The Corner Hardware Store" was the name of the business you had owned and operated for the last ten years in a southern city. As a neighborhood business you did
fairly well, never really making a huge profit, but well enough to be comfortable. Of
course there had been a couple of years when the economy was bad and your customers had to cut back on home projects, thus leaving you with some minor losses.
The business had picked up since then and you were running in the black.

As in many parts of the country, your area has experienced very unusual
weather this year. There have been a number of small floods and a major one. Just
last week, a tornado did heavy damage to your neighborhood. The results are that you
are experiencing very brisk sales as people begin to fix the damage done to their
homes. In fact, you are continually running out of some building supplies. Conse-
quently, you have been spending increased time trying to locate new suppliers and
working out shipment schedules.

Your sister, who is the bookkeeper for your store, has been trying to convince
you that this "building boom" is a golden opportunity for the business. She has suggested that because the market for building supplies and tools has created great demand, you should take advantage of that fact and boost your prices to increase your
total profit.

"You need to let the market dictate the prices," she told you. "After all, this
kind of a situation isn't going to last forever, is it? There are so many items you can
jack up the prices on because the customers just have to have them, that you can double or triple your profits while the demand lasts."

"That sounds kind of unfair to the customers," you responded.

"Why? Isn't supply and demand the name of the game? Isn't capitalism all
about making profit? The demand is much higher than the supply can satisfy right
now. To me that means higher prices will not cut down on sales and will bring in
some real money for a change," she replied.

"But we are making money already. It's not like we're in the red. Besides, this
sounds unethical to me. It is taking advantage of people's misfortunes to make a
larger profit. Most of the people coming in lately are neighborhood people whose
houses were damaged by the floods and tornado. I mean, they're really hurting. How
can I reap windfall profits off of their hardship?"

She just looked at you and shook her head. "Where were all these customers
those two years when we almost went under? Don't you think they know the situation? Most people understand that when supplies are short, prices rise. Look at what
happened during the gas crisis of the 1970s and the Gulf War. Gas prices went up
when the supplies were cut down. People understand this. Why not make a little extra
for us now? Besides, this certainly isn't illegal, so how can it be unethical? And remember, this little building boom isn't going to last forever."

You considered her arguments and had to admit they made some sense. There
was no law against raising prices to suit the circumstances. Many resort towns and
tourist-related businesses pumped up their prices during the busiest parts of the sea-

son. You knew a couple of towns up north where the locals stopped eating at the town restaurants in the summer because the prices went up so much during the fishing and camping season. Those same local folks came back and patronized the restaurants from Labor Day to opening day the next year. They understood the situation because many of them worked for businesses that followed the same practices. Everyone took it for granted that this was just good business. Maybe your sister is right.

Then again, this set of circumstances seems like a very different situation from "summer tourist season" price increases. Those tourists are there voluntarily and know ahead of time what kind of prices to expect. Your customers are having to re-build their homes after a series of disasters over which they had no control. This con-cern raises a couple of serious questions in your mind. First, is it ethical to make a profit by charging more to people who are recovering from a disaster? They have no choice but to rebuild and therefore are acting under a sort of duress to begin with. Is it fair to exploit them? Second, the price increases are unexpected and may cause hard feelings if the customers feel you are just milking them to increase your own profits. This might leave permanent resentment and cause them to shop elsewhere in the future, even if you lower the prices back to normal later on. In fact, lowering the prices after they've fixed their houses may just convince them that you don't care about them as people, just as customers who can make you some extra money. Given that this is a neighborhood business, alienating the community seems like a risky proposition. Don't you owe your regular customers more than this?

When you discussed all of your thoughts with your sister and the other four reg-ular employees, they all agreed that these were concerns to take seriously. But apart from trying to be as gentle as you could in raising prices, they all agreed it made sense under the circumstances to increase prices. One employee pointed out all the extra work you had done trying to locate more materials and tools for your customers. Shouldn't you be compensated for that, he had asked. Your sister simply repeated her earlier points about supply and demand, the legality of a price raise, and that the cus-tomers had to understand that shortages meant higher prices. She ended by saying that any customers who felt alienated and then took their business elsewhere were cus-tomers you probably couldn't count on if a big hardware chain store ever opened up nearby. She urged you to "Make it while you can without gouging the customers."

The two sides of this issue both have merit. There is something to the notion that capitalism is about supply and demand, that there is nothing illegal about prices being raised, and that many businesses do this sort of thing every year when tourist season rolls around. If all this is true, what is wrong with you doing the same? On the other hand, you have the feeling of "kicking someone when they're down" in the cur-rent situation. Is it right to capitalize on storm and flood damage? Can you afford to alienate your customers? Or do you have a right to make a legal profit regardless of the circumstances? It is true that this building boom can only last a short time. Who knows what the future of your business will be? Shouldn't you do as well for your-self and your employees as circumstances allow?

It seems that you must act quickly if you are to maximize your profits. How do you see this issue being RESOLVEDD? It's all up to you, but many other people will be affected by your decision.

45. CAN YOU AFFORD COMPASSION? ▮▮▮▮▮▮▮▮▮▮▮▮▮▮▮
Worker's Performance Suffers after Attack

At times you hated having chosen a career in personnel management, and this was one of them. The decision you faced was very difficult, raising so many legal and ethical issues that you wished you had stuck with art history back in college. To terminate a worker was never something anyone in personnel relished, but to terminate Sheila Pully was especially difficult even if it was necessary.

You work for Quickie Help, a staff-leasing company that provides workers for various businesses. The company specializes in high-tech and highly skilled office workers, even providing a money-back guarantee for any client who was dissatisfied with Quickie's workers. It was because of the high levels of performance required of all Quickie employees that Sheila was being considered for termination. Sheila's job performance has slipped badly in the last two months and her last assignment brought a complaint from the client to your attention. As a result of several of her errors, the client had lost close to $2,000 in business. Quickie had covered the loss, in compliance with its guarantee, and sent two other workers to the client to repair the damage. These two workers were paid entirely by Quickie. Thus, Sheila's errors ended up costing Quickie close to $4,000 in all.

Quickie's president ordered you to investigate and terminate Sheila if you felt it was necessary. Normally such performance would automatically mean termination. Sheila's case was not normal, though. She claims that her ability to work had been severely compromised by psychological problems associated with a vicious attack and rape she had suffered five months earlier. An armed attacker had broken into Sheila's apartment, overpowered her, tied her up while he robbed her, and then raped her before leaving her tied on the floor. A neighbor had discovered her two hours later. She was hysterical and incoherent at that time. With the help of her neighbor and friends she recovered from her physical injuries and some of the emotional trauma over the next two months before returning to work at Quickie. But the remaining psychological damage was proving very difficult for her to overcome.

Before the attack, Sheila had been very efficient at a variety of the types of jobs Quickie specialized in. She could operate a computer, keep books, run numerous financial and bookkeeping programs, and handle many secretarial tasks and some management jobs as well. In short, she was a very skilled worker and a valuable asset to Quickie. That was before her attack, however. Since returning to work she had displayed a number of lapses in attention, abruptly left two or three times a day, and had been discovered crying in the lunchroom on two separate occasions. All of this had happened in the first month and had taken place at Quickie's offices where she was being slowly reacclimated to the work environment. The management, after about five weeks, felt she was ready to go back to working with clients.

Her first job went reasonably well, but some of the effects you had noticed in her when she was at Quickie's office lingered. She had finished the two-week assignment without major problems. The client had rated her performance as "fair" on the evaluation form, noting that she seemed distracted and worked "kind of slow." Her second job was the one at which she cost the client and company $4,000. The client had complained that she just couldn't seem to work fast enough to get the jobs done by deadline times. When she did work fast enough there were many errors in her work. On the last two days of the assignment the error had occurred and the client had requested she be replaced. It seemed clear that she was not handling the post-traumatic effects of her attack very well.

Having consulted with Sheila and the company doctor, you have concluded that she is not likely to be back to her old performance levels any time in the near future, if at all. The stress of the deadlines and highly detailed work she is supposed to do accentuate her delicate emotional state, causing her to have what she calls "minibreakdowns" frequently. She feels that she can continue working, but you and the doctor have serious doubts about that. She might be able to handle less skilled and stressful work, but she surely cannot handle the kinds of assignments Quickie specializes in. Moreover, there are no other positions that she could be moved to within the company.

The doctor's final assessment, based on a series of interviews with Sheila, was "After the trauma Sheila experienced during the rape, she cannot continue to handle the stresses of her job without jeopardizing her mental health even more. I cannot foresee her maintaining the level of productivity required to handle her assignments. She may eventually recover, but it will be a long process."

Can you afford to keep Sheila at Quickie? What concerns you is not just the money she is costing the company. In the long run, what further expenses might result from the trauma accumulating from the pressures of her continued work? Sheila, on the other hand, maintains that she can do the job and is entitled to keep trying because she has been a valuable employee at Quickie for years. She believes the company owes her something because of that record. She also believes that firing her for the effects of a rape is equivalent to firing someone for a handicap and therefore might be illegal. On one occasion she had even suggested that if she were a man who had been mugged no one would be asking that she be fired. But because she is a woman who has been raped, a crime our whole society has often "blamed the victim for," she feels termination would be "the ultimate sexist act." You wonder whether she will sue Quickie on this basis if you terminate her.

You are reasonably sure, though, that given her performance lately, many employers would have terminated her sooner because of incompetence. Does the cause of the poor performance matter in the final analysis? Isn't just the ability to perform one's job the key factor? If it is, Sheila hasn't been performing and many people believe she won't be able to perform again at the required level. Is Quickie a charity or a business?

Your decision has to be made soon. The president is asking for your decision at the end of the week. Can you jeopardize Quickie's reputation by keeping Sheila on the payroll and sending her to clients? Because no in-house positions or any other low-stress assignments are available, termination for lack of performance seems the only reasonable alternative to taking the chance on her. But doesn't the situation merit some consideration for her? She is the victim of a brutal crime that was not her fault. She was a valuable employee before the incident. It may even be true that she has no control over her emotional state because of the trauma of the attack. Is it fair to fire her if her performance lapses can be attributed to these facts? Yet, you are the personnel manager for the whole company and her continued employment can harm the company.

These are the problems you must work through. What is ethical? Legal? Fair to Sheila? Fair to the company? Finally, what should you do in the case? The issues must be RESOLVEDD by the end of the week when you meet with the president.